CHICKEN SOUP FOR THE SOUL
CELEBRATING MOTHERS AND DAUGHTERS

CHICKEN SOUP FOR THE SOUL CELEBRATING MOTHERS AND DAUGHTERS

A Celebration of Our Most Important Bond

Jack Canfield
Mark Victor Hansen
Dorothy Firman
Julie Firman
Frances Firman Salorio

Health Communications, Inc.
Deerfield Beach, Florida

www.hcibooks.com
www.chickensoup.com

We would like to acknowledge the many publishers and individuals who granted us permission to reprint the cited material. (Note: The stories that were written by Jack Canfield, Mark Victor Hansen, Dorothy Firman, Julie Firman, or Frances Firman Salorio are not included in this listing.)

What's the Word? Reprinted by permission of Annette M. Irby. ©2006 Annette M. Irby.

The Truth. Reprinted by permission of Stephanie Welcher Thompson. ©2006 Stephanie Welcher Thompson.

Through the Fog. Reprinted by permission of Joyce Elaine Long. ©2006 Joyce Elaine Long.

My Adoption Day. Reprinted by permission of Rebecca M. Yauger. ©2006 Rebecca M. Yauger.

(Continued on page 299)

Library of Congress Cataloging-in-Publication Data

Chicken soup for the soul celebrating mothers and daughters / [edited by] Jack Canfield . . . [et al.].
    p. cm.
  ISBN-13: 978-0-7573-0590-0 (trade paper)
  ISBN-10: 0-7573-0590-3 (trade paper)
  1. Mothers and daughters. I. Canfield, Jack, 1944- II. Title: Celebrating mothers and daughters.
  HQ755.85.C4975 2007
  306.874'3—dc22

                                                        2006033441

Publisher: Health Communications, Inc.
        3201 S.W. 15th Street
        Deerfield Beach, FL 33442-8190

Cover design by Andrea Perrine Brower
Inside formatting by Dawn Von Strolley Grove

Dorothy and Frances dedicate this book
to their mother and coauthor, Julie,
who has been a lifelong inspiration.
Her eighty-seven years of loving wisdom
have guided and comforted more people
than we can count. Without her,
this work would never have blossomed.
We love you, Julie.

Contents

1. THE BOND BETWEEN MOTHERS AND THEIR DAUGHTERS

2. A DAUGHTER'S WORLD

3. TIME TOGETHER

4. TRIUMPHS LARGE AND SMALL

"We come 30,000 miles and all he says
is 'go ask your Mother.'"

Acknowledgments

We wish to express our heartfelt gratitude to the following people who helped make this book possible:

Our families, who have been chicken soup for our souls!

Jack's family, Inga, Travis, Riley, Christopher, Oran, and Kyle, for all their love and support.

Mark's family, Patty, Elisabeth, and Melanie, for once again sharing and lovingly supporting us in creating yet another book.

Julie's family, Winfield Firman, husband, father, grandfather, and great-grandfather, to whom she gives her love and thanks for a lifetime together; and Tom, Lore, Linsay, Ashley and Tim Firman, her son and his family, each of whom has made her life richer and more blessed.

Frances's family, Cynthia Salorio and John and Nicole Salorio, who bring joy and meaning to her life and make the world a better place to live.

Dorothy's family, Ted Slawski, husband, best friend, and soul mate, and her children and grandchildren: Jody Slade and his daughter, Sarah; Sarah, Chris, and Mia Rose Goodbar; and Thomas Slawski, bright and shining stars, each and every one.

All of us share in the hopes and dreams of our children as they and their families continue to grow in the coming years.

Our publisher, Peter Vegso, for his vision and commitment to bringing *Chicken Soup for the Soul* to the world.

Patty Aubery and Russ Kalmaski, for being there on every step of the journey, with love, laughter, and endless creativity.

Barbara LoMonaco, for nourishing us with truly wonderful stories and cartoons.

D'ette Corona, for being there to answer any questions along the way.

Patty Hansen, for her thorough and competent handling of the legal and licensing aspects of the Chicken Soup for the Soul books. You are magnificent at the challenge!

Veronica Romero, Teresa Esparza, Robin Yerian, Jesse Ianniello, Lauren Edelstein, Laurie Hartman, Patti Clement, Maegan Romanello, Noelle Champagne, Jody Emme, Debbie Lefever, Michelle Adams, Dee Dee Romanello, Shanna Vieyra, and Gina Romanello, who support Jack's and Mark's businesses with skill and love.

Michele Matrisciani, Carol Rosenberg, Andrea Gold, Allison Janse, Erin K. Brown, and Katheline St. Fort, our editors at Health Communications, Inc., for their devotion to excellence.

Terry Burke, Lori Golden, Kelly Maragni, Tom Galvin, Sean Geary, Patricia McConnell, Ariana Daner, Kim Weiss, Paola Fernandez-Rana, the sales, marketing, and PR departments at Health Communications, Inc., for doing such an incredible job supporting our books.

Tom Sand, Claude Choquette, and Luc Jutras, who manage year after year to get our books translated into thirty-six languages around the world.

The art department at Health Communications, Inc., for their talent, creativity, and unrelenting patience in producing book covers and inside designs that capture the essence of Chicken Soup: Larissa Hise Henoch, Lawna

Patterson Oldfield, Andrea Perrine Brower, Anthony Clausi, and Dawn Von Strolley Grove.

All the Chicken Soup for the Soul coauthors, who make it so much of a joy to be part of this Chicken Soup family.

Our glorious panel of readers who helped us make the final selections and made invaluable suggestions on how to improve the book: Rebecca Aronson, Gloria Ayvazian, Bobbie Behrens, Kathy Broderick, Jan Butsch, Michele Caprario, Pat Coscia, Edie Cuttler, Robin and Jillian Diamond, Michele Edelstein, Tara Gorvine, Jane Hutsles, Alex Leras, Nancy Noel, Bonnie Ortmann, Heather Perkins, Joyce Rapier, Nicole Salorio, Diane Smith, Dolores Steward, Holly Stiggleman, Carla Thurber, Alayne Vlachos, Heidi Washburn, and Donna Weeks.

And, most of all, our warmest thanks to everyone who submitted their heartfelt stories, poems, quotes, and cartoons for possible inclusion in this book. While we were not able to use everything you sent in, we know that each word came from a magical place flourishing within your soul.

Because of the size of this project, we may have left out the names of some people who contributed along the way. If so, we are sorry, but please know that we really do appreciate you very much.

We are truly grateful and love you all!

Introduction

My mother, Julie, is eighty-seven years old. My sister, Frances, and I are old enough to know better than to say how old we are. And all three of us are old enough to have spent most of our adult lives as mothers, all of our lives as daughters, many years of our lives as grandmothers, and for Julie, more than seven years as a great-grandmother. In this way we are like all women. While all women may not have been mothers, all have been daughters. All have had mothers. All have given of themselves, and all have loved and been loved.

Julie, Frances, and I are also psychotherapists, and as such, we have worked with thousands of women who bring to our offices and workshops the stories of their mothers and daughters: stories that all share the theme of love. No matter what the hurt, the deeper story is about love.

Since our first *Chicken Soup for the Mother and Daughter Soul* in 2003, we have been honored to receive hundreds and hundreds of stories from courageous, loving, humorous, wise, spiritual, hardworking women, young and old. Every story has touched us, and each story reminds us why we do this work.

Mothers and daughters are a strong and powerful thread in the tapestry of life. Woven throughout history, both public and private, are the stories of mothers and daughters doing their part to save and serve the world. Mothers raise the future. Daughters are the future. Together, sharing one another's stories, we will make the world a better place.

Dorothy Firman

1

THE BOND BETWEEN MOTHERS AND THEIR DAUGHTERS

Every mother has the breath-taking privilege of sharing with God in the creation of a new life. She helps bring into existence a soul that will endure for all eternity.

James Keller

"Mom and I have always had a special bond,
except in our choice of fashion."

What's the Word?

Children reinvent your world for you.

Susan Sarandon

There has to be a perfect title to use for my baby girl, a designation that will express what she means to me. I've tried nicknames, like "Cherub" or "Angel"—they're adorable monikers, but they're just not quite right. And then there's "Sunshine" because she does light up my days. This little one holds my heart in her hands, but I freely extend it to her because her love undoes me. She has captured me just by needing me so much.

There's another nickname I use, but my older girls wonder about it: "Baby Doll." I remember wrapping my beloved dolls in blankets and cooing to them when I was a child. Now the bundle in the blanket moves and coos back. No, "Baby Doll" doesn't quite fit. Then there's "Treasure Bear." She is one of my treasures. She is full of treasure. I adore her, my little five-month-old. Yet, she's not a bear, so I keep searching.

The usual terms of endearment are not quite specific enough—"Sweetie" or "Honey." Not quite.

She is a cutie-pie. She makes me laugh with joy, and I smile until my face hurts just trying to entertain her. She carries the future and reminds me of my childhood. She slobbers on everything and will soak the sleeves of her outfits from sucking on them. But that doesn't lend itself to a name.

I've varied her given name, which is fun, and those titles do stick, but they're not quite right. There must be a word to fully express everything she is—sweet, adorable, lovable and lovely, endearing, strong (oh, how she can communicate her dissatisfaction when necessary!), and gentle. She will take my face in her hands and bring her open mouth close to me. I know she's thinking, "If only I can get Mommy's whole face in my mouth, I will truly experience her!"

That's what I need, a title to sum up the experience of her. I love to enter her room in the morning, walk to her crib, and speak softly to her. I love how she calms at the sound of my voice. I love unwrapping the blankets that soothed her overnight, then scooping her up for a snuggle. How delightful to bathe her, dress her, sing to her, and rock her. How satisfying to feed her and know that as she grows I'm doing the right things. I love her response to my ministrations. She's just begun raising her hands to me. Oh, such rapturous joy! Sure, I knew I was one of her favorite people before now (such a delicious feeling), but suddenly she has the capacity to demonstrate it with more than a cry—with outstretched arms. Yea!

So what is the perfect term to express who she is to me? What her value is to me, and my love for her? There is a word. It's ideal. Yet, it's common, as natural as mothers and their baby girls. It's precious. It's a word that will never sound as dull as it did before my baby girl came along but will always shine with new glorious meaning. A word that teaches me my value even as I assign it to my little girl. It expresses a value that won't fade when she's as old as I am, my own mother's little girl. A special word with hidden meanings. What is it? WHAT IS THAT WORD? . . . Delight? . . . Joy? . . . Sunshine? . . . Not quite, not quite, not quite. . . . AHHHHH. . . . Now I know. . . . Daughter. That's the word I've been hunting for.

Annette M. Irby

The Truth

Sooner or later we all quote our mothers.

Bern Williams

I never yearned for a baby like some women do. Oh, I thought I'd have children eventually, but there were lots of other things in life that I wanted to experience first— achievements that seemed bigger and more important than someone simply calling me "Mom."

My own mother stayed at home with my sister and me until divorce drove her to find employment. She worked at the telephone company for the next twenty-five years. Mom's job always seemed dull to me. Consequently, we had a recurring conversation throughout my growing-up years.

"Mom, when you were a little girl, what did you want to be when you grew up?" I often asked, hoping I could discover what she really wanted to do for a career.

Each time, Mom hesitated before she answered. "All I ever wanted was to have children," she'd say with a smile and a faraway look in her eyes. "I just wanted to become a mother."

Try as I might, I never got a more satisfying answer out of her.

"But didn't you want an exciting career?" I chided. "Maybe being a nurse or owning your own business?"

"I only wanted to become a mother," she whispered, like she was sharing a precious secret.

As a child in the 1960s and 1970s, I failed to understand her desire. A record number of women were entering the workforce. But all my mom aspired to do was to bear children! There had to be more.

Instead of settling down after high school like Mom, I looked to hip, female role models who encouraged teenage girls, like me, to get careers and find themselves. Success was measured by a framed diploma on the wall and a professional position in the workplace. Marriage and children were for my mother's generation. There was a world of opportunity to explore. So that's what I did.

My theory was that anyone could become a mom, but not just anyone could travel to exotic destinations or have an adventuresome vocation. So, when I was twenty years old, I planned my career path and made a list of "things I want to do before I die."

Motherhood didn't make the cut.

I traveled the world, seeing sites in exotic locales like Europe, Australia, and Egypt. I worked in glamorous positions as a television news reporter, radio talk show host, and syndicated newspaper columnist.

Yes, my life might have been thrilling, but after becoming a first-time mom at forty-one, I discovered that my theory of motherhood being an ordinary experience was wrong. Nothing compares to the overwhelming love I feel for my daughter. Instead of occupying a desk chair to work after hours, I nestle in the rocking chair, coaxing two-month-old Micah to sleep.

Necklaces that can be pulled by tiny fingers, or earrings

that might scratch her face remain in the jewelry box. Tailored suits that need dry cleaning have been replaced by wash-and-wear clothing that won't show stains when the baby drools or a diaper leaks. Spit-up is an everyday occurrence. But I consider it my badge of honor.

Don't get me wrong. I'm glad I went to college and discovered my heart's desire in a professional career. But along the way, I wish I'd known that my mother's preferred profession of child rearing had merit, too.

Being a mom is the best position I've ever held. Watching my daughter grow and develop is more educational than any training seminar I've attended. Seeing her smile when I look into her face is more rewarding than any business partnership I've created. Introducing Micah to new toys and seeing her enthusiasm rivals hiking in the outback or exploring the pyramids of Giza. With a baby, every day is a trip into the unknown world of discovery and delight.

And it is more challenging than any college class I ever attended. The nasal aspirator had remained a mystery to me until one evening when Micah had an excessive amount of fluid in her nose. In order for her to breathe, I had no choice but to learn how to work the bulbous device and eradicate the buildup. It took about twenty minutes of concentrated effort on both our parts, but I finally achieved success.

About that time, my husband, Michael, came in from work.

"Honey," I hollered. "You've got to see this."

He walked into the nursery.

"I finally cleared the baby's nose!" I said, proudly displaying a tissue.

Michael did not share my elation.

At that moment, I knew I had officially moved from being a woman with a baby to being a mother.

Today I'm here to break the conspiracy of silence. The role of a mother is not to be belittled but rather exalted. Being a mom is an exciting career every bit as fulfilling as any other work in the world. Motherhood is the chance to assist God in creating another human being. What could be more important than that?

These days when someone asks me about my greatest achievement, I smile and get a faraway look in my eyes. Then I share the secret: "It's being a mother."

My mom was right all along!

Stephanie Welcher Thompson

Through the Fog

Sometimes the strength of motherhood is greater than natural laws.

Barbara Kingsolver

One glance to the left confirmed what I already knew. The speedometer's needle was well beyond the last mark. Interstate lights blurred as our V-6 Oldsmobile sped north toward the Eighty-sixth Street exit. A slight shimmy rocked the car as my husband, Al, steered past what appeared to be a huge eighteen-wheeler truck.

Seeing him hunched over the steering wheel struggling to see through the balmy October fog, I realized my intense Lamaze breathing was fogging up the inside of the car, too. Suddenly when pounded with another urge to push the baby, I swallowed a yell. Our childbirth classes had not covered waking up to daggerlike contractions two weeks early.

No longer could I sit comfortably. Stretching backward, I raised myself off our car's plush navy seat. Arms trembling to support myself, I could not help but think that something was terribly wrong with our second child, who was plunging quickly into our world. Two years earlier our son's birth was complicated by a tangled umbilical cord.

As we slowed slightly to exit the bypass, the urgent need to push intensified. Sweat rolled down my nose. Gritting my teeth, I swallowed the salty flow. By now I was crying. I could feel my baby coming. Fortunately, now we were within minutes of the women's hospital.

Because it was almost 2:00 AM, my husband wisely decided to run the three stoplights leading to the hospital. Soon we had parked in the curved canopy close to the front door. Al helped me slide out of the car and gently guided my shaking body to the front automated door.

An observant receptionist summoned an orderly who rolled a wheelchair toward me. At that point, my hysteria and pain merged.

"Don't make me sit! I'm having a baby right now!" I sobbed.

Through my fog, I saw a freckle-faced nurse trot out from behind two white doors. After her quick pelvic exam with me still standing bent over in front of the reception-ist, she intercepted my panic and began paging our doc-tor, whom we had telephoned just twenty-five minutes and twenty-three miles ago.

Immediately the small preliminary exam room behind the receptionist became crowded with an assortment of trays and scrub-gowned nurses. "We don't have much time, do we?" the groggy, unknown doctor confirmed. Later the auburn-haired nurse told us that she had awak-ened him from the nearby doctors' lounge. He did not even have time to put in his contact lenses.

Slowly he guided out what I was sure was a stillborn child because there was silence, no wailing like our son's first look at life. But then I felt the pulsing cord as someone laid him on my stomach. I was certain that this one was another boy, since all of my husband's older siblings had boys.

"A nice pink baby girl," a voice out of nowhere announced.

"Is she okay? Is she okay? How's her head? I want the Apgar score," I demanded. My mind could still see an umbilical cord strangling her.

"She's fine, really. You have nothing to worry about, Mrs. Long. Her Apgar rating is a nine, which is very good. Her cone-shaped head will reshape normally. She's a beautiful, healthy baby."

Al squeezed my hand and grinned.

"Now I can see," the stand-in Dr. King mentioned, now wearing his contacts. Al and I looked at each other, concerned but then focused on our chubby little girl being washed in her Plexiglas bassinet.

"You'd better camp out at our doorstep if you ever have another baby, Mrs. Long," the orderly teased as he scooted me onto a wheeled cart.

"You're determined to push me somewhere tonight, aren't you?" I said referring to our earlier wheelchair encounter. "By the way, where are we going?"

"To the delivery room, of course. You're going to pay for it so you might as well see it."

As the white doors closed behind us, our first nurse pushed the clear bassinet that held our daughter, who was quietly examining her toes. The orderly pushed me and the IV, while Al walked by my side. Then we saw our doctor.

"What are you doing here?" he asked.

"You know us. We couldn't wait. We had a baby," Al said to the kind, aging doctor who, in thirty years of practice, had never missed an on-call birth.

A few minutes later in the small but cozy mauve delivery and recovery room, Al and I took turns holding our seven-pound, slightly jaundiced daughter. With her chubby cheeks, orange coloring, and Columbus Day birth, her nickname soon became Pumpkin.

We wanted to telephone our family, friends, and neighbors but thought we should at least wait until dawn. For the first time since our high-speed trip, we thought about our two-year-old son, who was still semiasleep when we left him at our neighbor's house.

Over twenty-two years have passed since our daughter's dramatic entry into this world. Our Pumpkin is now a senior in college, living ninety minutes from home. Valerie Adele is still the only granddaughter on both sides of our family. And she would readily admit that she has been spoiled throughout the years because of this status. "But maybe not enough," she would add.

From wailing over a bad hair day to the classic rolling eyes during a lecture from Mom, our daughter has provided her fair share of drama since that foggy October night. One thing is certain, though. That evening was the only time in her life that she was early for anything. And, yes, we love her anyway.

Joyce Long

My Adoption Day

Hope is the parent of faith.

Cyrus Augustus Bartol

I was devastated as I left the attorney's office with my husband.

"I guess that settles that," I said as Vince opened the car door for me, and I slipped inside. He climbed into the driver's side but kept the keys in his hand.

"Settles what? We can still do this," he said.

"There's no way I'm going to ask Bonnie for that. It's not worth me legally adopting her if we have to order a new birth certificate with my name on it. She remembers her mother. Having a new birth certificate is like asking her to pretend her mother never existed. I won't ask her to do that." I couldn't stop the tears from welling in my eyes.

I had been married to my husband for two years. We had long since been talking about my adopting his teenage daughter. Her mother had been killed in an accident several years before, when Bonnie was ten years old. I had been so excited heading into the attorney's office to start the proceedings. Now my heart plummeted, all because of a piece of paper that would have my name on it.

"I know it makes sense when you adopt a baby," I told my husband as he started the car. "It just never occurred to me that Bonnie would need a new birth certificate at her age. I won't do that to her. I won't make her choose between mothers."

"Babe, just let me talk to her, okay? I'll tell her what's going on. She's been supportive up to this point."

"I know. But I think this is too much to ask."

"Let me talk to her. Trust me."

My husband squeezed my hand affectionately, and for his sake, I smiled through my tears. But in my heart, I knew my dream was finished.

I consoled myself by knowing this wouldn't change my feelings for Bonnie, and maybe we didn't need this adoption after all. I loved her, and she was the daughter of my heart. That would have to be enough.

Several days later, my husband sat me down.

"I talked with Bonnie," he began.

I looked at him, not understanding what he was talking about. My dream of adoption died the day we left the attorney's office the week before.

"About what?" I questioned.

"About the adoption. You'll never believe what she said."

I didn't reply, waiting for my husband to continue.

"I told her the situation about the birth certificate and how you felt about that. Her reply was, 'Why do I care what a piece of paper says? Mom wouldn't care what a piece of paper says. I want this to happen. I want Becky.'"

Tears poured from my eyes. I couldn't believe what I was hearing. Bonnie was choosing me. I knew I could never replace her mother, but I also knew that with the love I shared with her father, I was taking my place in their lives. And now I understood how much it meant to me to have this little girl call me "Mom."

The joy I felt as the adoption day approached was boundless. The day we went to court finally arrived. I looked at my daughter and asked, "Are you ready to see the judge?"

She looked at me, her blue eyes shining, and said, "Yes, I'm ready, because today, I'm adopting you!"

Rebecca Yauger

Three Moms—One Heart

*Mother's love is peace. It need not be acquired,
it need not be deserved.*

                                                          Erich Fromm

Recently our family celebrated our daughter's thirteenth Forever Day, the day we stood in court and promised a judge that we would love and take care of our daughter forever. It didn't matter what we told the judge or anyone in the courtroom; we belonged together as parents and daughter even without the legalities of the adoption.

Nearly fifteen years ago, we began this journey of parenthood, not in the way I had imagined so long ago when I stood at the wedding altar beside Richard and imagined our future together. And yet, the result of reams of paperwork, hours of parenting classes, home visits, interviews, and nerve-racking times of waiting was glorious.

Our Michelle arrived into our lives in mid-November and nothing was ever the same. For twelve years we'd prayed for the child of our heart. Richard and I knew we wanted children from the moment we decided to marry. Our plan was to have two children and adopt a third. The second part of our dream came true and overshadowed the loss of the first part.

Within a couple of weeks of the phone call telling us of the nine-month-old little girl waiting for us, we were sitting in the living room of her foster parents. Nothing had prepared me for the way I felt when my daughter crawled into my lap. Her name was Gayle Michelle. Richard and I had long ago chosen the name Michael or Michelle for our first child. I hoped she could get used to the name switch; we intended to call her Michelle.

"She's beautiful," I said.

Tina, her foster mother, smiled the same way I'd seen my own mother's smile of pride. She told me how smart my daughter was, and how friendly. That, I could see.

"She's wonderful. I can't wait for her to come home," I said quickly.

This woman who had raised my daughter for her first eight months of life stared at me, her smile disappeared, and I watched her expression change. She stood suddenly and let me know she had a box of clothes and toys we could have.

I realized how hard it must be for Tina to let go. And I realized how scared I was. Would Michelle like her new nursery? Would she love us, or be afraid? I wanted to cry. I turned toward Tina and saw that she was crying.

"She's like my own daughter," she whispered.

We stood at the nursery door, sizing up each other. I wondered if she resented me. I was surprised at the carousels decorating the nursery and explained that our nursery was decorated similarly.

"Michelle will feel at home," Tina said.

It was then I learned that they'd always called her Michelle. When I told Tina that we had long ago chosen the name Michelle, she smiled and grabbed my hand. "You'll really love her, won't you?"

"More than my life," I promised.

That was what she needed. Tension slipped away, and we were quickly giggling over photos and videos.

My daughter's first days of life had been traumatic: taken from her birth mother, drugs in her tiny body. But in reality, Michelle's first nine months had been blessed. She had the love of three mothers. One mother gave her life. Another gave her a loving home to wait in, and the third—me—would give her a mother's lifelong love and commitment.

For so many years I had cried out in pain, asking why we were denied the child we desperately wanted. And twelve years later, I was amazed at how the lives of three women had been lined up to bring us together through the love of one little girl.

A tiny girl who united three women's hearts in a special bond of motherhood, not limited by pregnancy and child-birth, instead bonded through our dreams for Michelle's future. A bond that knew no bounds and that had many years to celebrate her Forever Day.

Mary Kathryn Lay

Dandelion Bouquet

I got my first dandelion bouquet from my seven-year-old stepdaughter today. I dug out the sterling silver bud vase to put it in. You know, the vase that was a wedding present and has never been used. It is sitting proudly in the middle of the dining room table, and my husband knows better than to try to get me to move it.

Today I became a mother.

Last August I married a wonderful man and his three incredible children. I became a "bonus mom," and together we have been learning what that really means. In December my husband and I found out that we are expecting our own first child, and this August I will become a "birth" mom.

But today I became a mother.

What do those wilting yellow flowers mean? We spend so much time and money trying to rid our lawns of these weeds. How could a clump of broken stems and wilting weeds, held in the sticky hands of my seven-year-old, suddenly become more beautiful than expensive roses and professionally constructed bouquets? What magic transforms a handful of weeds into a heart full of love?

Sunday is Mother's Day, that annual tradition of home-made cards and special gifts made in church and school. I know my husband has taken the kids shopping for me, and I will be thrilled and surprised by whatever they have found for me.

But today, because of dandelions, unsolicited and from the heart, I became a mother.

Jessica Adam

I Can't Remember

My pregnant friend complains of a backache and tired
   feet.
"Was it like this for you?" she asks.
I bury my face in your newborn hair
And I answer, "I can't remember."

I hear a new mother talking of her sleepless nights.
"Does everyone go through this?" she wearily says.
I watch you tottering on your fat little feet
And think to myself, "I can't remember."

"When will he learn to eat on his own or tell me his
   needs?" A frustrated mother laments.
I look into your three-year-old eyes, gleaming with independence.
When it got there, I can't remember.

"These two-year-old tantrums are driving us mad!
How did you cope?" an exasperated couple inquires.
I watch as you happily skip off to school
As I murmur, "I can't remember."

"My teenager rebels at everything! He won't even keep his
    room clean!
What did you do with your adolescent?" a burdened par-
    ent entreats.
I look around at your unused room, everything in place
And sigh, "I can't remember."

You hand me my newborn grandchild, and with a beam-
    ing face you announce,
"Oh, Mom, he's so wonderful! Did you ever feel this way?"
I hold him close, and with tears in my eyes
I breathe, "Oh, how I remember!"

Barbara Nicks

On the Teeter-Totter

"I don't want to be like you. I just want to be like myself!" my daughter raged.

I knew this was coming. Everyone said it would. I just didn't expect it for at least another ten or twelve years. My daughter was two and a half when she declared her independence. I had forty years and a hundred pounds over the two-foot-nothing, twenty-five-pounder that stood defiantly in front of me. Yet, she took me down like a Sumo wrestler. Wasn't I supposed to be her universe? *Wasn't I supposed to be her everything?*

They say to be careful what you wish for you because you just might get it. Somehow I knew that in parenting Zoë, I was definitely in for a lot of "it." Time, that's what I wish for. Just a little time. I thought, *What about preschool?* Two days a week for three short hours each day. Perfect for an only child. She'll learn about holidays, and how to take turns; she'll get to play with all that messy gooey stuff, and I'll get to go to the gym and do errands without bringing toys or dealing with tantrums or fragrant, full diapers begging to be changed when I'm next in line.

"Preschool will be fun," I said, preparing my daughter, as if she needed that.

By the third week of the new routine, Zoë practically leaped out of the car as we pulled up to school.

"Wait up," I said, scurrying to catch up and hold her hand, but she balled it into a fist, pinned it to her side, turned and gave me the shoulder.

"You wait here, Mommy," she said. Then with her tiny index finger, she pointed to the precise spot on which I was to stand while she walked into the classroom—alone. She took several steps before turning back. It wasn't that she had second thoughts—she just wanted to make sure I hadn't moved.

While other mothers inside the class struggled to remove crying toddlers who were clinging to their legs, I was outside trying to sneak an inch closer to mine.

"You're so lucky," they'd say, adjusting their clothes as they raced for their cars. My "Yeah, I guess" was drowned out by the roar of gunning engines.

Pick-up time was no different. If I saw Zoë before she saw me, she'd just flat-out pretend I wasn't there. If she saw me approaching, she'd hide. Aside from feeling like a stalker, I was truly crushed.

"Is she mad at me?" I'd ask the teachers. "Is she trying to punish me for leaving her?"

"No." They'd smile. "She seems quite well-adjusted, happy, and involved—just very independent."

Had I forgotten about all those noble qualities I had prayed for in my child—hoping she'd be curious, self-sufficient, adventurous, independent? It's not that Zoë never needed me. In fact, there were plenty of times she couldn't get enough of me—like when I was in the bathroom, or on the phone, or sleeping.

So, for years we struggled to attain that perfect teeter-totter balance between my need for her and her need to be her own person. Invariably it was I who landed with a thud when I didn't get it right. Sooner or later I would have to face the truth: My child was born fuel-injected and destined to fly. In the meantime, all I could do was work on my balance.

It didn't seem like seven years from the playground teeter-totter to the Mother-Daughter tea, but there we were suddenly preparing for this big-girl event. The second grade teacher asked each mom to bring in an old childhood photo so we could try to match the present day mom with her past. As Zoë and I sorted through the pictures, my own second grade portrait slipped out.

"I don't remember that dress, Mom, when did I get it?"

"Sweetie, that's not you."

"Are you sure? It looks just like me. Who is it, then?"

"Honey, it's me when I was in the second grade."

"It is! Oh my gosh, Mom," she said, looking in the mirror with the picture next to her face. "We look exactly the same! Do you have any more pictures?"

"Well, here's one when I was about fourteen," I said, passing her the photo.

"Mom, you look really cute in that bikini. Seriously, you do!" she said, lifting her shirt to examine her belly button. "Do you think I'll look like that when I'm fourteen?"

Hah, was this a trick question? She said "that." Did she mean me? Did she actually want to look like me, or like herself? Once again I was back on the teeter-totter, wondering how many more thuds I had left in me.

"Maybe a little," I said, biting my lip. "But you have your own style—you always have, plus you'll probably end up cuter."

We teetered for just a moment.

"That's too bad." She suddenly slumped. "I really hoped I'd look just like you."

Tsgoyna Tanzman

The Ties That Bind Her

Nothing you do for children is ever wasted. They seem not to notice us, hovering, averting our eyes, and they seldom offer thanks, but what we do for them is never wasted.

Garrison Keillor

It was time.

Now that graduation was over, Katrina would be heading to college. Twelve hours away. In Idaho of all places. As I loosened my apron strings, I needed my firstborn daughter to take along a piece of home. A slice of her life. A healthy serving of . . . memories.

She would be sharing a diminutive dormitory suite with five other girls, so I knew there was no room for the burgeoning, bulky binders I'd filled; her seventeen years worth of scrapbooks would reside at our house for the time being.

So, how? What? There had to be some other way to snag the past and send it along. And then it came to me: The Idea. I'd create something special out of the one thing that hadn't gone into her scrapbooks—her wardrobe.

"Katrina," I hollered up the stairs, "I need your help."

When I explained my idea, her enthusiasm matched my own. "That's great, Mom. Let me go see what I can round up."

While Katrina searched her room for odds and ends, I headed to the basement corner where a teetering tower of boxes resided. Old jeans. I'd saved them for the "someday" when I'd try my hand at a denim quilt. Someday had arrived.

Unfolding a bent cardboard corner, I opened the flaps and reached in.

"These aren't hers," I muttered and lifted down another box. "Ah-ha!" I pulled out pair after pair. My excitement mounting, I sorted through the remaining boxes, thrilled at the treasure trove I discovered.

Stone-washed.

Acid-streaked.

Ticking-striped.

I made a pile of bibbed overalls—all from her preschool years. I set aside Levi 501s—with buttoned fronts. I noted welted side seams here, contrasting topstitching there. This pair had embroidered pockets. That pair, zippered ankle sides. And the colors, why I'd never realized the variety of blue hues from brand to brand and after multiple washings. Surely there was enough here to. . . .

"Good grief!" Katrina's exclamation interrupted my mental calculations. "I wore all these?"

I looked up. "Yep. And wore some of them out. Look here, the knees are gone in this one."

"Why, I remember those." She poked at the intricate, basket-weave pockets. "Everyone in fifth grade owned some." She pointed at the elasticized ankles on another pair. "And those. Oh my goodness. I loved wearing those at clogging competitions."

And so together, the two of us—my maturing daughter

and I—planned the quilt that would cover her bed at college. Katrina donated the intricate details and finishing touches: slick, patterned hair ties from her ponytail era; leftover eyelets and laces from her girly stage; and name-brand labels from her favorite tees and tops—her peer-pressure period.

She added comical knee patches and odd Girl Scout badges. She harvested quirky hardware and textural straps from dated belts, out-grown shoes, and old backpacks. She unearthed a Cabbage Patch pendant and a Barbie doll bangle.

And she helped me stitch them on, one memory at a time.

The end result?

"Perfect," I admitted.

"A masterpiece," she insisted.

We backed the patchwork top in a downy flannel plaid. We threaded two blunt needles with strands of crochet floss and marked the center of each denim square.

"Let's start tacking them from the middle of the quilt on out," I suggested.

Katrina nodded her agreement and we set to work, securing the sections with a back stitch and cutting the thread ends to precise lengths. And all the while, I smiled within, knowing I was also securing my firstborn daughter to her past even as I was cutting her loose to embrace the future.

Carol McAdoo Rehme

Our Hands

*Thou art thy mother's glass, and she in thee
Calls back the lovely April of her prime.*

William Shakespeare

Bright and tasteful, red nail polish tipped my mother's slim fingers, smooth to my touch. As I snuggled next to her on the sensible yellow couch in the living room of our 1950s Ossining home, she read to me from the big Hans Christian Anderson storybook. As I became the ugly duckling floating across to the next page now in her full essence of swan, my mother's red-tipped fingers absent-mindedly rubbed the back of my hand.

We are connected; you belong.

My mother did her own nails once a week. Curled beside her, I watch as she dips the slender cap-brush into the bottle, removing just the perfect amount of polish and artfully applying thin strips until the entire nail is covered, not a drop lost or out of place, like the most accomplished painter. Decorating herself so, my mother used the craftsmanship she applied to her meticulous, detailed architectural drawings as she sat over the large slanted drawing board in the shadowy alcove of her bedroom.

I hold out my hand.

"Do me, Mommy."

With reverence, excitement, and total surrender, I rest my small hand on my mother's lap. Into the bottle dips the same slender brush. My mother starts with my child-thumb. My piano teacher says that I have perfect hands for piano playing. Little does he (or I) know that these hands are not destined for the cold, hard, black-and-white keys of the piano, but rather for contacting deep knotted spots in people's bodies, places that have become twisted onto themselves, stopgaps to the natural life flow. These hands were meant to open physiological spaces, where my mother's opened people's living spaces.

My mother focuses intently on my little hands, with a steadiness worthy of a neurosurgeon and with such care it is almost sacred. One by one I watch each nail light up with a vibrant glow that matches my mother's delicate but strong hands. Her hands that craft the entire inside of a house on paper, hands that cut a raw chicken, hands that could pull a hot dish from the oven. "Get back," she would warn as she reached for a steaming pot. "I can do this because I have asbestos hands."

My mother's hands would reach for mine in her late 'eighties when she was losing her sight due to an infection from a simple cataract surgery, resulting in repeated visits to the doctor for injections directly into her eye.

"Your hands give me strength," she whispered into my ear as we sat in the doctor's waiting room, her now frail hands holding mine, her red-tipped fingers absent-mindedly rubbing the back of my hand.

Heidi Washburn

Three Squeezes

To us, family means putting your arms around each other and being there.

Barbara Bush

I drive while trying to keep myself detached from the woman in the passenger seat. She is my mother, and she is mumbling about people doing "this, that, and the other," as she puts it. None of what she's saying is positive. She is having a cranky day.

"Good," I think. "That makes it easier."

I'm taking her to her day-care center, the place she hates more than any other on Earth. It is a day-care center for people with Alzheimer's disease.

To make the painful drive easier, I perform what has become my driving ritual. I begin to imagine a brick wall going up between us. She talks her nonwords, strings of them, not making any sense at all, and I add brick after brick in my mind. I want the wall tight and secure. If it becomes weak, I start to remember her the way she used to be, the way she should be. And then I can't do what I need to do. How could I take her someplace she doesn't want to go? So I try to forget who she is, much as she has forgotten who I am, by adding the bricks and driving on in silence while blocking the tempting memories from my mind.

But then she does something that crumbles the wall and crumbles me. She reaches over and grabs my hand. Before I can pull away she squeezes it three times. One, two, three . . . and the wall comes down.

Ever since I can remember, my mom and I have had our secret squeeze. One squeeze for each word: I love you. She squeezed to give me courage on the first day of school. She squeezed to give me reassurance when I was a teenager and didn't want to hear her words. She squeezed to tell me she was sorry when we'd had an argument. She squeezed to say, "That's the one," as we looked at the white wedding gown in the window. And she squeezed when words stuck in her throat as I handed her a baby girl named Ellen. I love you. Silently. Just between us.

The wall torn down, I turn to face her. She says to me, "You're such a pretty girl, do you know that?"

The words are hard for her. Sometimes they come out wrong or go places she didn't intend.

"I'm not sure who you are," she says.

I tell her that I am her daughter. She looks surprised. I tell her that the baby in the back is her grandson.

This is the one act I don't mind performing in the drama of Alzheimer's. Every time I tell her that she has grandchildren, her eyes light up with tears and sometimes she squeals like a little girl in utter delight. She looks at him, as if for the first time, and he waves his two-year-old hand at her, used to the routine, used to the woman-child who is his grandmother.

"Oh, I wanted one of those!" she says. "I wanted one of those!"

I tell her that she had babies. I tell her that I am her baby and she is my mother. She looks confused. She says my name, and I'm relieved she's remembered it. But she is confused as to who I am, nonetheless.

"I used to be your baby," I tell her. She laughs because this is funny to her.

"I don't know. I just don't know," she says. "But I have loved you forever." And then three more squeezes.

The tears come freely for me now. This causes her concern. Her brow furrowed, she rubs my hand.

"What's the matter? What can I do?" she says.

She sounds just like herself. Hopefully, I turn to face her, but with one quick glance I can see she's not there. She begins talking nonsense, about "those people" and all that they do wrong.

The magic settles and I start to rebuild the wall. I stop, however, after a couple of bricks. Instead, I reach over and grab her hand. I squeeze it three times. She smiles at me and says again, "You're such a pretty girl. I have loved you forever."

She is sincere. She could pick me out of a crowd of thousands. She wouldn't know who I am, or be able to connect me with the baby that floats in and out of her memories, but she'd know that she's loved me forever.

Three squeezes. Her way of telling me that all is not lost. Her way of telling me her heart has not forgotten. Her way of telling me, of all the things she did in her life, I was the most important.

Carol Pavliska

"Don't Go"

Our society must make it right and possible for old people not to fear the young or be deserted by them, for the test of a civilization is the way that it cares for its helpless members.

Pearl S. Buck

As a little girl, I remember being attached to my mother. I was told that when I was about three years old, when my mother was ready to leave for work, I'd wrap my little arms around her neck and say, "Don't Go!" Of course, she'd reassure me that she'd be back in a little while, but to me each minute seemed like an eternity. When those words of consolation didn't work she'd try the good old, "I'm going to make money so that I can buy you toys" trick. Well, my older brother would rub his little hands together and shrill at the mention of the word toys. As for me, the single most important thing that could make me happy was, of course, my mother.

Looking back, I'm quite thankful that her working days were short-lived. (I'd like to think that it was due to my persistent demand.) Over the years, her patience, love, and words of wisdom have been such a blessing to me. Now that I have three lovely daughters of my own, I'm more deeply touched by that special bond, unspoken, yet quite divine, that exists between mothers and daughters.

Last summer my mother, at the age of seventy-three, unexpectedly needed open-heart surgery. Prior to this, her last hospital stay was forty-six years ago when I was born. She was now in congestive heart failure and could barely breathe without an oxygen tank. Her valve was quite narrow, and she had an aneurysm in her aorta as well. Although I was no doctor, I knew what this meant: Surgery was the only option if she wanted to live. I quickly learned how involved pre- and postsurgical procedures would be, but I had to be strong for her, like she had always been for me.

The entire week before surgery I did not leave her side; I was even allowed to sleep in her room. It was a special time for both of us. We reminisced about our family, especially her eight terrific grandchildren, and had many heart-to-heart talks as we watched the sun rise and set over the George Washington Bridge. The lights on the bridge sparkled like diamonds each night, appearing as if its large expanse was almost touchable from her room-with-a-view. As her surgery date approached, my heartfelt mission was to keep her in good spirits and a good frame of mind to face this major operation.

The day of surgery arrived. We sent her off with lots of hugs, kisses, and reassurances as we held on to her gurney, traveling through halls, onto an elevator, and into the pre-op station.

Before we knew it, we were in the waiting room. Like many of the families around us, we shared in camaraderie of watching the clock. Whenever surgeons walked in, time stood still. Each family understood the exhaustion, anticipation, and the silent prayers from the heart as we huddled closely within our own little worlds, on couches, on chairs, sitting around tables drinking coffee, talking, reading, sleeping, waiting . . . just waiting . . . to hear the proverbial words, "Everything went well!"

About four hours later, we stood up anxiously, finally seeing the surgeon. We listened with bended ear as he explained that the surgery went well, as expected. "She should be in the recovery room shortly," he reassured us. "So wait for the call." A sigh of relief overcame us all as we sank back into our chairs. *So now we just wait,* I thought to myself as I glanced at the phones on the wall, each labeled with a different medical unit. These phones were now the lifelines to our loved ones. When the phone rang, silence swept through the waiting room as someone nearby would quickly answer it, then call out the family name. This would tell us when our loved one was in recovery and we could begin our "Five minutes on the hour visit." Name after name was heard as we anxiously waited. Two hours had gone by and still no word on my mom. *What was going on?* I wondered as I paced the floor, much like an expectant parent. I finally called the recovery room, only to find out that she was not there yet. Now panic set in as my mind reeled out of control.

Finally at 3:30 that afternoon, we were informed that there were complications as they were closing, and she was placed on bypass for the third time. The thought of losing my mother was overwhelming. I needed some air! My tears turned to sobs. This was the worst day of my life!

It seemed like an eternity, but our name was finally called after ten-and-a-half long hours of waiting, so we rushed over to the Surgical Intensive Care Unit. I froze in the doorway, almost afraid to walk in as I saw this frail figure hooked up to several machines. *Mothers are invincible,* I said to myself as I walked closer, blinking back the tears. Post surgery is difficult for family members because, although we're told what to expect, no one is prepared to see a loved one in that condition. As we left, I kissed her forehead and whispered, "I love you, Mom!"

The next morning as the nurse drew back the curtain, my mother was awake. Her eyes met mine. She wanted to speak but couldn't because of the tube in her throat. We told her that she did really well during the surgery and that she was going to be fine, so she should just rest now. After five minutes, the nurse reminded us that time was up and we could come back in an hour. As we were leaving, my mother motioned for a pen. With the amount of anesthesia that she had the day before, I never expected her to be able to write. I watched her intently as she took her time, diligently forming the letters that read "Don't Go!"

I gently lifted the paper to show the nurse, we smiled at each other then looked at my mom. From that very moment on, that sweet nurse allowed me to stay with her for as long as I wanted every day. I could see that she, too, understood that the special bond between mothers and daughters requires no explanation. Day by day, my mom got stronger. An amazing recovery by all means!

About a month later, as I was cleaning out my pocketbook, a white note fell onto the counter. As I unfolded the paper, my mouth curled into a smile and a tear filled my eye as I read the sweetest words "Don't Go!" carefully inscribed on that small piece of paper. Those words will forever be engraved on my heart, treasuring the special bond that I share with my mother. I realized then that this simple yet profound request had come full circle, that I had honored her urgent and heartfelt request as she once, long ago, honored mine.

Mamie Amato Weiss

2

A DAUGHTER'S WORLD

In search of my mother's garden, I found my own.

Alice Walker

Okay, Mom, I Confess

Okay, Mom, I confess,
I broke the kettle, I made a mess,
I spilled chocolate sundae on my dress.
I was the one who spilled dirt on the rug,
broke your TV, and your mug.
I sort of accidentally forgot to feed your fish,
and also accidentally, I broke your favorite dish.
Mom, there's just one more thing I have to say,
do you still love me anyway?

Lydia Paiste, age nine

I Love You More

Love will find a way.

English Proverb

Meet my daughter, Amanda. Four years old and a fount of knowledge. The other day she was reciting a list of all the facts and tidbits she has memorized: One plus one is two. If you mix yellow paint with blue you get green. Penguins can't fly. . . . On and on she went.

Finally, she finished. "Mom," she said, looking very smug, "I know everything."

I let on as if I believed her but chuckled to myself thinking of all the this and thats a four-year-old child couldn't possibly know. Comparing her four years to my almost three decades of life experiences, I felt sure I knew what she knew and then some.

Within a week, I'd learned I was wrong.

It all began as we were standing in front of the bathroom mirror, me fixing Amanda's fine, blond hair. I was putting in the final elastic of a spunky pair of ponytails and finished with, "I love you, Amanda."

"And I love you," she replied.

"Oh, yeah?" I taunted. "Well, I love you more."

Her eyes lit up as she recognized the cue for the start of another "I love you more" match. "Nuh-uh." She laughed. "I love you the most."

"I love you bigger than a volcano!" I countered—a favorite family phrase in these battles of love.

"But, Mom, I love you from here to China." A country she's learning about, thanks to our new neighbors up the street.

We volleyed back and forth a few favorite lines: I love you more than peanut butter. . . . Well, I love you more than television. . . . I even love you more than bubble gum.

It was my turn again, and I made the move that usually brings victory. "Too bad, chickadee. I love you bigger than the universe!" On this day, however, Amanda was not going to give up. I could see she was thinking.

"Mom," she said in a quiet voice, "I love you more than myself."

I stopped. Dumbfounded. Overwhelmed by her sincerity.

Here I thought that I knew more than she did. I thought I knew at least everything that she knew. But I didn't know this.

My four-year-old daughter knows more about love than her twenty-eight-year-old mom. And somehow she loves me more than herself.

Christie A. Hansen

Creative Mothering

Imagination is the highest kite that can fly.

Lauren Bacall

When I was a little girl, I was lying on my bed in the middle of the day with my door closed and nothing to do. I don't know what possessed me, but suddenly my big, clean white sheet was calling out to me like a large blank canvas, so I looked around my room until I found a pen.

Since this was back in the sixties—the era of flower power and paisley print—I began decorating my sheets. A vivid arrangement of flowers, stars, spirals, swirls, snails, and mushrooms began to emerge from beneath my pen. I was happily lying in the midst of all my favorite doodles.

Obviously, this was somewhat akin to drawing on the walls, and not likely something I was supposed to do, but in my young mind, it would probably come out in the laundry, so I didn't think it was a big deal.

How wrong I was! It was a BIG deal.

There I was contentedly drawing away when the door to my room opened. I must have been too quiet in there, and Mom decided she had better check on me. I looked up, guilty as could be. My cheeks flushed as I dropped the pen, knowing that I had been caught red-handed drawing on my sheets. There was no way to deny what I had been doing.

Of course, as any mother would, my mom ordered me to stop immediately. She left the room and came back a few minutes later with something in her hand. Then she came over, sat down on my bed, and said, "Please don't draw on your sheets—unless you are using permanent markers! I don't want your artwork to wash out. You are an artist!" There before me on the bed, she placed an assortment of colorful permanent markers.

My life's journey was nurtured then, and many times after, by this creative mother who knew the things that were truly important.

Eve Eschner Hogan

The Secret

Faith is the only known cure for fear.

Lena K. Sadler

Ever since I can remember, Thanksgiving meant piling into the car and driving over to have dinner with my extended family. After dinner, while most everyone sat around the table laughing and digesting, a few of us began cleaning up. As we carried piles of white china across the room into the waiting kitchen, we reminisced. Auntie talked about some of the things we did when we were kids that were cute, and then we laughed about some of the not-so-cute things my cousin did as a teen.

"I never had to worry about you, Helaine," my mom announced, loudly enough for all to hear. She was using the booming voice she always used when she was going to embarrass me. It echoed around the room and bounced off the vaulted ceiling of the dining room.

"You were a good kid. You didn't get into trouble, you didn't do drugs, you did well in school. I never had to worry about you."

My thoughts wandered back to high school. I

remembered one particular summer, between my junior and senior years, when I thought I was beyond the control of curfews. My parents felt otherwise. So whenever I went out, I would be welcomed home by the soft buzz of the fluorescent light glowing above our kitchen sink, reflecting off the white tiles on the walls. It was a sign that even though Mom and Dad were sleeping, they were really waiting up. They wouldn't—or couldn't—rest until they heard the tumble of the deadbolt in our kitchen door and saw the light above that kitchen sink turn off. It didn't matter what time I came home; my parents knew exactly when that moment was.

One evening in late July, when it was so hot that the nights didn't cool off, I went out with some friends. We were on our way to the beach to hang out and watch the sunrise, when I realized that curfew was coming. I had a dilemma—miss curfew, or miss sunrise. It was then that I hatched a plan.

About two minutes past curfew, I ran up the blue wooden steps leading to our entrance. Walking in, making enough noise to be heard, but being quiet enough to be considerate of my "sleeping" parents, I turned the deadbolt into the door with a "thunk" and switched off the glow above the sink. In darkness, I felt my way to the bathroom door, where I turned on the water and made "getting ready for bed" noises. A quick walk to my bedroom, and then— without shoes, but in white stocking feet—I slid across the white and brown linoleum floor, careful not to pause on any critical squeaking areas. I slinked down the kitchen hall, past the table and chairs, to the door. Somehow I managed to open that kitchen door in absolute silence and shut it again behind me even more quietly.

That was it! I was free! Off I ran to my waiting friends, to the beach, to the sunrise, to another night of my youth. My parents were none the wiser.

So there I was, age thirty-five, with this deep secret of mine. I wasn't really a good kid.

After my first success, I had attempted and succeeded several more times that summer to elude my parents and play all night long. Eighteen years after the fact, I felt it was time to share my secret with my mother, now that it was safe. As I told my story, my mother listened quietly and patiently. When I finished, Mom decided to tell me a secret of her own. Her secret told me more about my mother than I had ever known before. Her secret made me become determined to be like her when my own daughter becomes a teenager.

She wrapped her arms around me, and as she squeezed me, she smiled and shared her secret.

In my ear, she whispered, "I know."

Helaine Silver

The Unexpected Gift

Giving frees us from the familiar territory of our own needs by opening our mind to the unexplained worlds occupied by the needs of others.

Barbara Bush

Like many little girls, when I was young I could be found rummaging through my mother's closet. It was one of my favorite pastimes to step into her shoes, try on her silky blouses, and prance around the house with her pocketbooks. At five years old, I wanted to grow up and be just like her—a beautiful stay-at-home mom who made everything from watering the flowers to cleaning the house a grand adventure. I was blessed with a wonderful childhood and even better memories.

But my perfect little world changed the summer before my senior year in high school. I woke up one morning, like any other day, making plans to hang out with my friends when I heard a knock on my bedroom door. It was my father, who had stuck his head in to say, "Amanda, your mom and I would like to have lunch with you today. Can you meet us at eleven thirty?"

Having lunch with my parents wasn't at the top of my priority list, so I was less than thrilled. "Well, Laura and I were going to go shopping. Can we just see each other tonight?" I asked. "No, we have some good news, you'll be glad you came."

My dad shut my door, and I could hear his footsteps walking down the hall.

"Good news?" As I drove to the restaurant later that day, all I could think about was the "announcement" they had to make. *Were we going on vacation? No, we had already been to the beach that summer. Did we have company coming?* There were people in and out of our house all the time, family and friends; that wouldn't be a big deal. *Could they be giving me my graduation gift early? That was it! I was getting the red convertible I had been asking for, for over two years!* The more I thought of it, the more I convinced myself I was getting this shiny new red car! As I pulled into the parking lot, my heart beat faster and faster as I started eyeing the cars lined up row by row. I could see my parents' Buick in the distance. *Would they have parked my new gift close by?*

I was practically walking on air as I spotted my mom and dad sitting at a table close to the window. They were holding hands, which I usually would have thought was gross, but on that day, the day I was getting my new car, I thought it was kind of cute. As I sat down beside them, I couldn't hold it in any longer, "I can't wait! Tell me what it is! What's your big announcement? What is it?"

I sat up straight in the chair and was just about to put my hands out for the keys, when they both said simultaneously, "We're having a baby!"

"What?" I gasped. Before I could even process what was just said, I blurted out to my mother, "But you're too old to have a baby!" When in reality, she wasn't even forty yet.

I could see my mother's eyes begin to water, her chin start to tremble, and I was sure at that point, they were serious. Our family of three was soon to become a family of four. I knew my mom had always wanted more children. When I was younger she had lots of tests and procedures done, but the doctors had all said the same thing, "We're sorry."

I drove home that day in my eight-year-old Nissan, knowing that our life as we knew it would never be the same. The mother who had held a washcloth over my head when I was sick and who served countless cups of imaginary tea to me and my stuffed animals would be changing in every way. The memories that she and I had made over the last seventeen years she would start making with our new baby. Just as I was about to leave my parents' house, they would be introducing someone else to the world.

The next nine months flew by. Between planning for homecoming and prom, we painted a yellow nursery and bought baby blankets. We celebrated graduation parties one weekend and baby showers the next. It was a whirlwind filled with anticipation and excitement! When the day we had been waiting for finally arrived, we welcomed Jake III into our family. He was a beautiful, healthy baby boy and the best graduation gift I could have ever received.

Most people know if they have a great mom. I not only know it, but I get to see it all over again.

Amanda Dodson

My Eight-Year-Old Teenager

*Parents can only give good advice or put them
on the right paths, but the final forming of a person's character lies in their own hands.*

Anne Frank

Like most parents, I fantasize about having a loving,
nurturing relationship with my child. So during the first
seven years of my daughter's life, I tried to follow all of the
recommendations from the top childhood experts. I spent
quality time with her at interesting places, used positive
reinforcement and praise to build high self-esteem, and
created a strong family bond by fostering a sense of love
and togetherness. I also taught her how to play a mean
game of jacks.

I imagined us, when she got older, being like a family on
the cover of a magazine or on a television sitcom.

Then she turned eight.

Now, there is nothing really wrong with being eight. I've
always thought of it as a nice, nonthreatening age, except I
can't get used to the fact that one moment my daughter is
hosting a tea party with her dolls, and the next, covering

most of her body parts with temporary tattoos. I was caught completely off guard until a close friend explained to me that "eight" isn't really an age at all; it's more of a holding pattern between childhood and adolescence.

At first I tried to ignore the early signs—like her refusal to hold my hand when we crossed the street, or her request that I stop standing up in the bleachers and yelling things like "BUBBLE GUM AND TOOTIE FRUITY, WE GOT THE POWER TO WHOOP YOUR BOOTIE! YEE HAW!" during her soccer games.

I finally got the message when she began interrogating me on our way to her new classroom for third grade orientation.

"Mom, I don't want to hurt your feelings," she said. "But you aren't going to wear your long denim skirt again, are you?"

"Yes, in fact, I am. Why?"

"Oh, no reason," she said. "But you're not going to wear the matching floppy hat with the big silk flowers, too. Right?"

"Well, I was considering . . ."

"Or the Birkenstocks."

"But—"

"And, please, don't go and ask all those questions about things like grades and stuff, okay?"

"Well, I—"

"You know," she said, matter-of-factly, "my desk is real small and it would be hard for you to sit in it wearing a long skirt and all. But there are a lot of bigger chairs in the back of the room." She smiled brightly.

The more she talked, the more I grew suspicious that a teenager had somehow invaded the eight-year-old body of my little girl. After all, how could this be coming from the same person who, since she was three, thought I was the prettiest, coolest, and smartest person in the world?

This couldn't possibly be the same girl who once insisted on wearing her fairy princess costume, accessorized with a pair of furry pink plastic high heels and a purple feather boa, everywhere she went for six months.

Or the very child who had, just the other day, looked up at me with both arms outstretched and shouted, "Turn me around and spin me, Mom!"

I finally arrived at her classroom: a broken, silent, hatless woman wearing a pair of plain jeans and modern shoes. I obediently sat in one of the "big chairs" in the back of the room along with the other hatless parents and tried to look as if I didn't actually know anyone in the third grade—I had just wandered in off the street to take a little rest.

As the school year progressed, I wasn't sure how I felt about the two versions of my daughter, especially since I could never be quite sure which one I was dealing with.

Like the time I sat down in the recliner and was stabbed by a bottle of contraband Fire Engine Red nail polish. I waited until my daughter wasn't looking, then carefully slipped it into the trash. Two days later I found it in the bathroom behind the soap dispenser. So I hid it in my medicine cabinet. She put it on her dresser. I stuffed it into the big garbage can in the garage and gloated over my parental victory. Then she fished it out and painted it on her toenails.

Shortly after that, she came home from school, put one hand on her hip, and announced that if anyone should need her, she would be upstairs in her "apartment" doing her homework.

At first I didn't know what to make of it. Then I decided to go along with it, since referring to her bedroom as her apartment would make the rest of the house mine, at least in theory, without having to wait ten more years.

I fantasized about sitting all alone in my spotless living

room, wearing my long denim skirt and floppy hat, belting out songs like "Tie a Yellow Ribbon Around the Old Oak Tree" with all of the windows open. And standing up to shout soccer cheers anytime I felt like it. Or being able to watch all of the talk shows and listen to seventies music on the stereo. Maybe even dance!

But as she closed the door behind her, I wasn't sure if I was ready for all that freedom yet. Especially since, deep down, I can hardly believe the baby I used to crochet sweaters for wants to wear designer jeans and trendy shoes. I feel sad thinking that upstairs, in her eighty-five-square-foot pastel pink apartment, my daughter is lost somewhere between fairy tales and training bras.

But occasionally my little girl returns.

Like the other day when, after three hours of not speaking to me because I wouldn't let her wear lipstick to school, she looked at me with big, innocent eyes and asked me to tell her again what color gown the tooth fairy wore—and what exactly she did with all of those extra teeth. And if I was "absolutely sure" that she would be able to find our house, much less the tooth hidden underneath her pillow.

I smiled and reassured her, like so many times before, that the tooth fairy couldn't possibly miss our house, since it was the only one on the block with Christmas lights on it in July. I told her, once again, that the tooth fairy wears a translucent blue gown with silver glitter sparkles and a magic golden crown. And definitely no lipstick. And I explained that she flits about collecting teeth strictly as a hobby. Her real job is being the chief executive of a lucrative denture company, which she earned by doing her math homework without her mother telling her and going to a good four-year college. But I can tell that she doesn't really believe me.

In fact, I almost expect her to blurt out "No way!" lunge

for my lipstick, and announce that she has, at last, found a bigger apartment in a trendier neighborhood and will be moving out on her own first thing tomorrow morning.

But instead she stretches her arms up to me and shouts "Turn me around and spin me, Mom!"

I smile, then put my arms around her and hold her tight as we spin.

Debbie Farmer

Drawing the Line

You can learn many things from children. How much patience you have, for instance.

Franklin P. Jones

Nothing warms a mother's heart more than observing her adult daughter shoulder the mantel of motherhood— and parent her own daughter. I sit back and smile as I watch Kayla juggle the "But why?" questions, deal with tantrums, and trip over toys. In a blink of an eye, it seems, what was once my life is now her life.

But I especially enjoyed the teaching moment I witnessed one Sunday after church. My daughter was strapping her toddler into the car seat when she paused to examine a dimpled knee.

"Oh, my goodness, Avery. What did you do here?"

"I drawed on my weg," replied her artistic two-year-old.

"You drew on your leg," Kayla corrected as she rubbed at the marking pen lines with a damp thumb.

"I drew on my weg," Avery replied agreeably.

"Leg, Avery. Say 'leg.'"

"Weg."

"No, l-l-l-leg." Kayla's tongue overemphasized the consonant as she fastened the seatbelt.

"W-w-w-leg," she repeated, with some frustration.

"Try again, Avery," her mommy persisted. "Say 'l-l-l-leg.'"

"W-w-w . . . Knee!" My granddaughter said firmly. "I drawed on my knee!"

There are some grins a mother just can't hide.

Carol McAdoo Rehme

True Giving

My daughter was six or seven years old when it happened, when she taught me a lesson I have never forgotten. It was early December, the day she and her classmates were asked to bring something to school to be given to children who might not be receiving any Christmas or Chanukah gifts. The children were told it was fine for them to offer something of theirs they no longer played with rather than something store-bought.

That evening just before dinner, Naomi came into the kitchen with her favorite doll—the one who slept by her head every night, with the flushed cheeks and the soft braids of brown fleece, the color of Naomi's hair: Molly. She handed her beloved doll up to me saying, "Molly can be another little girl's friend now." Then pushing Molly up a little higher into my reluctant arms, as if she knew she needed to convince me, she said, "Molly wants to be another little girl's friend, a little girl who is waiting to love her."

I was maybe three heartbeats from intervening, from coming between well-worn and well-loved Molly and the unknown little girl who almost had her, between my daughter's intention and its being carried out. How hard for me to let go of that handmade doll with rosy cheeks and no features except for two stitches for eyes, so her moods and expressions could be imagined—created—by the child. Molly, who looked like she was breathing, too, when Naomi closed her eyes each night yielding to sleep, always the one Naomi greeted first each morning—how could I give her to a stranger? I did not say that, did not call the girl to whom Naomi was giving her favorite doll, just a stranger, but I did ask Naomi if she was sure that she wanted to give Molly away. As if my daughter were confused instead of enlightened, I gently tried to turn her attention to the others, like the bear with the blue button nose (also one of my favorites, but at least not number one), or maybe the creamy white elephant, watching myself hope it would be one of the nameless ones that we would not miss—no, that I would not notice missing.

But Naomi stood so clear offering up the one dearest to her saying, "Momma, this is the dolly I love the most. So she is the best one to give."

I knew she was right, more deeply right than the reasoning and grasping of my "mature" mind.

Naomi gave Molly away. And to me she gave a lesson in generosity I have not forgotten, not yet living it as she did that morning except perhaps in the continual letting go of her, the one I love so deeply—a woman now, living three thousand miles away—giving herself to her life and to those waiting to love her.

Ani Tuzman

3

TIME
TOGETHER

*Some things are very important and some are
very unimportant. To know the difference is
what we are given life to find out.*

Anna F. Trevisan

In the Middle of the Night

Sophie calls out from her bedroom across the hall and my eyelids spring open instantaneously. I've been in the thick of dreams, but their complex storyline vanishes immediately in deference to the waking reality of my daughter's cries. I take a deep breath and look at the clock. In the dark of our bedroom, its cobalt blue digital numbers are the only source of light. It's 4:15 AM and my mind immediately does the math—that's nine hours of sleep for my eleven month-old—another banner night! I throw off the body-warmed quilt, glancing momentarily at my sleeping husband while listening to his steady breathing. Another cry from Sophie and I'm up.

When I open her bedroom door, I find her sitting up in her crib. I start humming the little melody I wrote for her just after she was born. I guess I consider it our "theme song." During the first months of her life, I have sung this melody over and over again, sometimes with words made up in the moment, sometimes with just the melody. I offer it as a musical anchor—a familiar mantra repeated over and over that wordlessly says to her "Mama's here!" It's a way that my voice can reach across the room to embrace her until I can hold her in my arms.

Sophie hears me now, and her cries quiet immediately.

When I reach into her crib, she stretches her sleep-warmed body toward me. Sophie looks a little dazed, in between the worlds of awake and asleep, but she still flashes me her beautiful smile. "Mama's here." I whisper the words to her now, as I carry her over to the small wicker couch.

At 4:15 AM the sky is still completely black. There is no moon. The silence wraps around us like a thick wool blanket. We are cradled in this soft stillness. I lift up my shirt and Sophie takes easily to my breast. Her sucking is slow and gentle as she lies completely relaxed in my arms. While she nurses, she reaches for my other breast with her free hand. I bend my head toward her to smell her skin and hair. There's a faint trace of chamomile from last night's bath and a little salty sweat mixed in with the sweet scent of her baby flesh. It's impossible to describe this scent in words but I know that every doting parent knows exactly what I'm talking about. There is nothing like the smell of your own sleep-warmed child.

I lean back into the cushion of the couch and close my eyes, feeling the familiar tug on my breast. The door creaks open and our male cat, "Kitty-Boy," slithers into the room. He always seems to know when we're nursing. In a flash, he jumps up on the couch, settles next to my hip, and starts purring. He stretches out one paw so that it touches my thigh. I can't blame him for wanting to worm his way into the warmth of our bodies. Even the cat knows that this is pure magic. I stroke Kitty Boy's head with my spare hand and his purring grows louder. The room practically pulsates with this tender, sleepy intimacy—mother, baby, and cat.

I stare at my daughter in her fleece pajamas with amazement, my heart overflowing. There are still moments when I feel stunned that I am a mother. For so many years—all of my twenties and most of my thirties, I thought that this would be somebody else's life—not mine. But here I am at forty-four, with my precious baby in my arms, sitting in the dark quiet of the middle of the night. I am wise enough to know to savor this moment completely—soon enough she will be weaned and all of this will be behind us forever. Even though part of me craves a night of unbroken sleep, I know I will grieve when these wee hour nursings come to an end.

Soon Sophie's sucking rhythm starts to slow down and it is clear that she is drifting toward sleep once again. Gently, I carry her slowly to her crib and lay her gently on her sheepskin. Her face is the picture of total contentment, her beautiful bow-shaped lips, her cheeks with a hint of rose in them. As I gaze down at her, I know I am standing as close to purity as I ever will during my time on earth. I cover her with her quilt, raise the side of her crib and head back to my cozy bed. My husband stirs as I get in. I nestle up behind him, spooning his warm body. Our fingers intertwine. I listen to the rhythm of his breath as I allow sleep to overtake me.

Sara Elinoff-Acker

Nice Hat, Lady!

To appreciate life, share it with others.

Austri Basinillo

Being the mother of three sons, I never had the experience of having a daughter. I figured that my opportunity to have my girl would only happen when one of my sons got married, and then I would become a mother-in-law. And what kind of a relationship would that be? Would I be the dreaded mother-in-law that everyone jokes about, or would my daughter-in-law and I be close? You never know what will happen. But when my son Mike got married, I found out.

I lucked out! I got a wonderful daughter-in-law named Crescent. We like each other and enjoy being together. And we do laugh—a lot. Sometimes our laughing gets us in trouble. Crescent decided she wanted to go to beauty school and become a hairstylist. How nice for me! The program she chose was quite demanding. Besides the book learning, she had to work on clients—both men and women—who came into the beauty school to have their hair cut, colored, permed, and styled. In exchange for a reduced price, these people agreed to be worked on by the students. It was a learning experience. And that could work out to be a good thing or a big mistake. But to support her dedication, I decided I would become one of her clients.

I had never been to a beauty school before, but I made my appointment. Crescent knew I was coming, so she was out in the lobby to greet me when I got there. I know she was nervous. Not only was she new to the profession, but she was going to be working on her mother-in-law's hair. Talk about stress! I was a little apprehensive, too, but we both decided that if we didn't like the results, it was not permanent and it could be corrected. No big deal.

So, the adventure began. Crescent led me back to her station and sat me down. One teacher came over to us and helped us pick out a hair color on the chart that best matched my existing medium brown color. Crescent mixed the dye and went to work on me. I sat for the time required for the color to take. And then we went to the shampoo bowl, and Crescent washed the dye out.

Why didn't she look me in the eyes? Was there a problem? That would be a good guess. Her face said it all. Her beautiful blue eyes were shocked at what she saw, but she didn't say a word. She just kept washing and washing. I had the cleanest hair in town. Finally she sat me up, wrapped a towel around my head, and walked me back to her station. The unveiling was about to take place. Yikes! My hair was black. Jet black! What had happened to my medium brown hair color? It was gone, and in its place was the blackest hair you have ever seen. It just sat there on my head and looked awful. Really awful!

One of the clients at the beauty school walked by my chair and said, "Nice hat, lady." And he was right. It did look like a hat. And a really bad hat at that! The only thing that was missing was one of those huge feathers sticking out.

Well, Crescent looked at me and I looked at her. And then we both started to laugh. It was not one of those polite little tee-hee laughs; oh, no, we were absolutely hysterical. Every time one of us would start to calm down the other would burst out laughing and the whole laughing thing would start all over again. Everyone in the place was looking at us—and that made us laugh even more.

Eventually we did calm down, and Crescent told me that she would take care of the problem. To fix me up so that I could go out in public, Crescent did a weave and put lots of beautiful blond streaks in my hair. I loved them! And they toned down the black color so that it was not that noticeable at all. Now it was okay for me to go out in public again.

The next time I had an appointment with Crescent, she lightened up the black color back to my medium brown color, but she has left those blond streaks in. We both decided that we liked the way they looked, and I still have them today. That was over seven years ago, and I have not been to another stylist since. We even had fun the time she put one pink streak in my hair—but that's another story.

Barbara LoMonaco

Always by My Side

Power is the ability to do good things for others.

Brooke Astor

I was scheduled for major surgery at a large medical center hundreds of miles from home to remove a tumor inside my head. I knew the routine well, for I had found myself on the receiving end of the surgeon's scalpel at least a dozen times in my forty years. But this surgery was different. My mother's health was failing and this would be the first operation I'd undergone without her by my side. Mother and I shared a common genetic condition, neurofibromatosis, and while blessed with loving friends and other family, our bond was like no other.

As I rode the tram from the hotel to the hospital for my preoperative workup, I'd never felt so alone in my life. *Oh, how I miss my dear, sweet, faith-filled mother,* I thought. My mind traveled back to all the times she'd eased the terror and uncertainty of having an incurable illness.

But Mother had done more than just make the ordeal bearable. She packed lunches chock-full of comfort foods for us to enjoy on the long train rides to the medical center. Her quick wit and outgoing personality assured that the hours, though difficult at best, would pass more quickly, and that we'd meet some new friends to boot. And how real God seemed when she prayed!

As I blinked back tears from loneliness and a blinding headache, an idea popped into my mind: Act like Mother and everything will be all right. Next thing I knew, I'd offered my seat to a man who grimaced as he clutched his side, and I'd all but forgotten my private pain in the process. When we departed the tram, I helped a lady who was burdened down with a bulky stack of x-rays. Her black hair was pulled into a tight ponytail, and a look of worry creased her face. It turned out we were both alone and having surgery the next morning, and as we headed toward the preadmission desk together, I asked God to help us both.

Suddenly, Mother's peaceful presence was absolutely palpable, and I understood, perhaps for the first time, the very heart of motherhood. For isn't that what mothers everywhere do all their lives—prepare their children for the difficult days when they can't be with them in the physical realm, and point their paths toward God, who will always be there with the greatest comfort of all.

Roberta Messner

Bra Day

Common sense is the knack of seeing things as they are, and doing things as they ought to be done.

Harriet Beecher Stowe

Bra Day is a not-so-annual family event that originated when my daughter, Cayce, was entering her freshman year in college. Heaven only knows how long she had looked frumpy underneath. When she finally pulled me into her bedroom, however, to exhibit her array (or shall we say disarray?) of loose and limp undies, we knew it was time to activate a new tradition in our family. We called it Bra Day.

"Face it," I told her. "There comes a time when a girl's underwear just totally wears out. All of it. All at one time. Bras, panties, slips . . . everything!"

Admitting she was in dire need of a makeover down under, we agreed the time had come to celebrate . . . in a big way. In preparation, and for some unknown reason, I actually looked up the word dire in the dictionary. The definition was spelled out clearly in just three profound

words: adj. Calamitous; dreadful; terrible. It was a significant description and so convincing that I got out the
checkbook to review the balance in our emergency savings account.

The next order of business was to ordain a shopping
day. Not just any day would do. This was going to take
some time. Initially, we would check out the newspapers
for upcoming sale specials, comparing the "Two-for-One"
ads against the "Buy Three, Get One Free" coupons. Then
we would take a day off work, arriving at the mall as soon
as they opened. We'd celebrate a larger size if necessary,
rejoicing in the growing wonders of womanhood. We'd be
cautious to spend wisely . . . that is, unless we saw something ravishing, in which case we had plans to splurge.
And, yes, we even proposed a special lunch to mark the
occasion . . . someplace new, maybe popovers at Neiman
Marcus.

My son shook his head as he overheard us making an
itemized shopping list, but we forged ahead. There were
decisions that had to be made. Cayce definitely needed
some new bras, but she also needed slips—a half one, a
whole one, a white one, a black one. She was desperate for
undies . . . and stockings . . . and socks. Everything was
worn out, too old to go on with life. The idea of a shopping
spree was turning into a gala affair, a jubilee of sorts. We
were pulling out all the stops. New lingerie was on the
way!

When the big day finally arrived, my daughter and I
headed for the mall. We started at one end and worked our
way to the other, searching through all the stores for
unadvertised specials to suit our budget. In the privacy of
each dressing room, we made our decisions from a prom-
ising combination . . . lacy see-throughs, conservative
three hookers, the practical and the padded, the low-cut
and the revealing.

I was the go-between, running back and forth to the racks, exchanging sizes, and confirming prices. She did the trying-on, barely giving me a peek, while I grappled with the tags and shoulder straps that were tangled in the hangers.

Bra Day was everything it was intended to be . . . and more. It was more than just an outing to replenish a girl's wardrobe. It was an outing to replenish the friendship between a mother and her teenage daughter. It was more than sharing lunch at Neiman Marcus. It was sharing secrets in the dressing room, spending Dad's money generously, buying more than we should have, and shopping till we were tired silly. It was laughing on the way home about how our cups runneth over . . . literally. It was throwing out the old and filling the drawer with the new. And it was just the beginning.

Over the last thirteen years, there have been other Bra Days. There was Bra Day on Miracle Mile in Chicago, where we "hooked" up for a weekend to shop for the bride-to-be. There was Bra Day in St. Louis, where we hunted for maternity shops in tucked-away places and came home with a bag full of nursing bras.

Now, I can promise you one thing for sure. I may not be there, but there will come a day when my daughter will take her daughter on her very first Bra Day. She will tell her about the calamitous situation she faced as a seventeen-year-old and how she and her mother solved it . . . together.

I may not be there, but I can promise you it will happen. Cross my Heart!

Charlotte Lanham

The Birthday Boots

"Ooooh, I like your boots!" my mother exclaimed, poking her head into the hallway. I had just walked into the house for a visit and was easing my feet out of a pair of brand-new red cowboy boots. A Christmas gift from my husband. "Aren't they cool? Try 'em on, Mom!"

My mother hesitated. "Well, okay." She wiped her hands on a dishtowel and picked up the shoes. A moment later she pranced into the kitchen, a smile on her face.

"These are nice! Comfortable, too."

"You should get a fun pair of boots like these, Mom. They aren't cheap but they're worth every penny!"

"Yeah?" Mom began removing the shoes. "I really couldn't spend the money on something like that." I had heard her repeat similar statements many times, a mantra honed by years of working to support four children.

I watched my mother place the boots by the door. She was dressed in a pair of bright yellow sweats that matched her fluffy blond hair. Mom loved wearing cheery colors. Sometimes I wondered if they helped her stay optimistic despite the worries and challenges of life.

Even after we were grown and out of the house, Mom

frequently put aside her own desires to give things to her children and grandchildren. Like the time she had come to see me when I lived on the East Coast. I was pregnant with my second child and finances were tight. There was no money for maternity clothes. Instead of spending her money on souvenirs, Mom surprised me with a shopping trip to buy some outfits that would fit my expanding shape.

On the drive home I thought of all the sacrifices Mom had made over the years. And not just to give her children the essentials, but to give them what they needed to flourish. As a child I had enjoyed an expensive hobby—horses. Born with that mysterious and obsessive gene called "equestrian," I pleaded with my parents for a horse almost from the time I could talk. Finally they relented and bought me a pony. That was just the start. After the pony came a string of horses, lessons, tack, a horse trailer, and shows.

I peeked at the toes of my new red boots and remembered when Mom had taken me shopping for riding boots as a child. I wondered how many things Mom had given up for herself to cater to my passion. She and Dad still worked hard. Even at age sixty, retirement was out of sight.

Mom loved horses, too, but had never had the opportunity to indulge her cowgirl fantasies. I could remember only one time I had ever seen her on a horse, though she showed me childhood photos of riding an aunt's horse, "Rocket." It wasn't until I was an adult, buying my own horses, that I questioned her in depth about it.

"Was it fear that kept you from riding, Mom?" It was hard to imagine fear getting the best of my positive mother.

"Sure it was fear," Mom answered. "If I fell off and got hurt I wouldn't have been able to work. I just couldn't take that chance." She fell silent. I was too sad to ask any further questions.

A couple of months later, it came time for Mom's sixty-first birthday. I made a mental list of all the things I could buy for her. She always needed clothing and loved to garden. I drove by a local nursery and looked at the baskets of flowers and garden tools. There were several things she would enjoy receiving, but one thing kept coming to mind: cowboy boots.

At the tack store I took some time looking over the many styles and colors. There were rows and rows of cowboy boots in all the regular colors and many I had never considered. I inhaled the clean, wholesome smell of new leather. One pair caught my eye. They seemed to have Mom's name on them. Bright cornflower blue and lime green with rubber lug soles. The boots were fun and spunky. Just like Mom.

I purchased the boots and a pair of Levi's jeans to go with them. Mom had never owned a pair of Levi's. I grinned, imagining my mother—now a grandmother— wearing her first pair of cowboy boots and Levi's jeans.

Mom came over for dinner on her birthday. After we enjoyed some ice cream, she opened up her gifts. Her eyes widened in surprise. "You didn't!" I followed Mom to the bedroom to watch her try on her new boots and jeans. She stood in front of the full-length mirror and stared happily at her reflection in the glass. "Well, aren't they the cutest things!"

"The boots are perfect for you, Mom," I told her, with a smile.

It was a special evening of food, conversation, and celebration. Celebration of a very special woman. Looking at her filled me with gratitude for all the things she had shared with me. Her love, her time, her resources. Even her horse-loving genes.

Maybe next birthday I'll take her riding.

Catherine Madera

Justine

Dogs are miracles with paws.

Attributed to Susan Ariel Rainbow Kennedy

I am busying myself in an unfamiliar kitchen, unpacking boxes. Since I am still reeling from my father's death, tears fill my eyes with every item I unwrap. Here we are, moving my mother into a new home—the home they had planned to live in after his retirement. My heart is heavy with sorrow. My mind is unsettled and filled with questions. *What are we doing here? How are we all going to manage? What happens next?*

"Quick! Come here!" It's my mother shouting from another part of the house. As I'm running to find her, thoughts of another tragedy race through my head as swiftly as my pulse races through my veins. "Over here!" I follow her voice out the front door. "Look at this!" Suddenly, from behind a small huddle of dogs on the neighbor's lawn, a little puppy charges full at me. Flashing deep brown eyes stare with singular purpose. Rippling multicolored fur flies about in furious waves. She springs into my arms and I am captured.

READER/CUSTOMER CARE SURVEY

CG3F

We care about your opinions! Please take a moment to fill out our online Reader Survey at **http://survey.hcibooks.com**.

As a **"THANK YOU"** you will receive a **VALUABLE INSTANT COUPON** towards future book purchases as well as a **SPECIAL GIFT** available only online! Or, you may mail this card back to us and we will send you a copy of our exciting catalog with your valuable coupon inside.

First Name _____ MI. _____ Last Name _____

Address _____

State _____ Zip _____ Email _____ City _____

1. Gender
❑ Female   ❑ Male

2. Age
❑ 8 or younger
❑ 9-12   ❑ 13-16
❑ 17-20   ❑ 21-30
❑ 31+

3. Did you receive this book as a gift?
❑ Yes   ❑ No

4. Annual Household Income
❑ under $25,000
❑ $25,000 - $34,999
❑ $35,000 - $49,999
❑ $50,000 - $74,999
❑ over $75,000

5. What are the ages of the children living in your house?
❑ 0 - 14   ❑ 15+

6. Marital Status
❑ Single   ❑ Married
❑ Divorced   ❑ Widowed

7. How did you find out about the book?
(please choose one)
❑ Recommendation
❑ Store Display
❑ Online
❑ Catalog/Mailing
❑ Interview/Review

8. Where do you usually buy books?
(please choose one)
❑ Bookstore
❑ Online
❑ Book Club/Mail Order
❑ Price Club (Sam's Club, Costco's, etc.)
❑ Retail Store (Target, Wal-Mart, etc.)

9. What subject do you enjoy reading about the most?
(please choose one)
❑ Parenting/Family
❑ Relationships
❑ Recovery/Addictions
❑ Health/Nutrition
❑ Christianity
❑ Spirituality/Inspiration
❑ Business Self-help
❑ Women's Issues
❑ Sports

10. What attracts you most to a book?
(please choose one)
❑ Title
❑ Cover Design
❑ Author
❑ Content

FOLD HERE

Comments

Do you have your own Chicken Soup story
that you would like to send us?
Please submit at: **www.chickensoup.com**

"She's so cute," I squeal. "What's her name?"

"We don't know," the new neighbor replies. "We found her in the bushes down the street, and she didn't have a collar. She can't be more than a year old. We posted ads in all the local stores and even in the newspaper, with no response."

"What a shame. How could this happen? But it looks like she's found a good home now."

"Oh, no, we can't keep her. We have three dogs of our own. We're taking her to the pound today."

Without thinking I blurt out, "You can't do that! She's so adorable. Can I have her? Please?"

For a long moment, he scrutinizes me. It seems an eternity before he gives an answer.

"Well, I guess it's okay. She really seems to have taken to you."

"Oh, thank you, thank you. I'll take very good care of her."

I glance down at the furry bundle nestled against me. Those eyes are still gleaming and centered on mine.

My mother asks, "What will you call her?"

Looking up in search of inspiration, I catch sight of the street sign. It reads "Justine Court." "That's it," I proclaim. "I'll call her Justine."

The following few days are spent locating a vet and groomer, buying a collar and leash, purchasing tags and toys, finding the right bed and food, and all that goes with settling a new member of the family. My mother, sister, and I are fully absorbed in each day's events. Justine lifts our spirits by giving us a loving focus amid the emptiness and confusion we feel. When we awake each morning feeling a hole in our hearts, her warm and devoted greeting gives us hope. When we return home from shopping or some other mundane outing, her jubilant, spontaneous exuberance gives us joy. It is a gift we need desperately.

We are a very happy little family until it comes time for my sister and me to leave. Our jobs beckon. I think it would be a good idea to leave Justine with Mother for companionship, but she insists that I take her with me. I don't protest.

Almost a year later, my mother suffers a massive stroke. My sister and I spend countless, painful hours in the hospital wondering if she'll live, followed by endless, agonizing days wondering if she'll ever recognize us again. Finally, the doctors say that nothing more can be done. I refuse to believe it. There has to be a way to reach her. We try writing down our names, reminiscing about important milestones in her life, bringing objects from her home. Nothing works.

Then one evening, as a last resort, I sneak Justine into Mother's room. At first, it's like all the other things we've attempted. There is no spark of remembrance. Gently, Justine nudges her face up into Mother's and stares wistfully into her eyes. I ask, "Do you know the doggie's name?" Inexplicably, Mother begins to mumble, "Justine—it's Justine." Soon, we hear our names, too. It is the beginning of her recovery.

Justine came to us from nowhere, although I suspect someone's hand placed her purposely in our path. Somehow, I feel that I saved her life, and in a way, she saved mine. I know she saved my mother's.

JoAnn Semones

Graduation Day

The elevator to success is out of order. You'll have to use the stairs . . . one step at a time.

Joe Girard

I woke up early. Rose-colored light streaked through the window as I lay still and savored the beginning of a special day. I heard the whirring of the air conditioner, soft snores from a room away. I told myself to close my eyes and sleep. But my mind wouldn't let me. It had taken more than three decades to arrive at this moment. Now we were here. In a few hours, my mother would walk across the stage, beautiful and proud, and claim her bachelor's degree.

I was at her home in Pittsburgh. There, in that cozy space alive with pictures and the scent of her vanilla perfume, my childhood always seems so close, like I can just walk out of the door and step into the past. I saw an adolescent me padding to Mom's bedroom and peeking through the crack at her studying a phone book–sized textbook. After working a full-time job as a data-entry operator, fixing dinner, helping me with homework, reading my younger brother a bedtime story, and making sure we were asleep, only then did my single mother sneak some time for her dreams.

I never questioned why she stopped taking classes. Just one day, Mom quietly tucked her college books away and planted her hope in my brother and me. She attended every piano recital, every open house, and spelling bee. She worked overtime to pay for summer trips and children's theater tickets. She became chauffeur for me and my friends, driving us downtown for shopping trips, to Junior Achievement meetings and teen clubs.

I thought about her sacrifice as the meaning of this day settled on me. She deferred her dreams so I could pursue mine. She cleared the way so I could soar, though her own path hadn't been easy. After a while, I heard Mom stirring. I headed into the hallway. Her smile lit up her face. Her eyes shined with hope. We hugged.

While she washed up, I laid out the dress I had bought her the day before—a flouncy black-and-white number—and flopped on her bed. I remember Mom treating me to a crimson and cream polka-dot dress for my college graduation ceremony. It was payback time.

When Mom slid on the dress, she whirled and looked like a dream.

"Kel, can you believe it?" she said excitedly.

I grinned in affirmation. On my special day, I felt the same. Breathless with anticipation. Choked with emotion. Overflowing with memories of how I got there.

On the day I was to leave for Syracuse University, my mom was short on cash. We had no money to pay a fee that was due when we arrived. Mom desperately phoned friends, family, called in every favor she had. My heart sank as my prospects of going to college that semester seemed to dim. But Mom's will was steel. She got in her car and didn't come back until she had a loan from her credit union. Late that night, we crammed into her silver Nissan Sentra loaded with my belongings and headed out on I-79 bound for Syracuse. Now, here we were, at another turning point, together again.

As Mom donned her black graduation gown, I held back tears. I knew how hard she worked for this moment. I knew how many times she had put her own needs on hold to give to my brother and me. I knew how often she had celebrated our successes. Now, it was her time to be honored.

My sister-in-law and I drove to Mom's graduation together. My nieces chattered in the backseat. I peeked at their innocent faces. Did they know they were about to witness history? We entered the hallway of Soldiers and Sailors Memorial Hall and saw a line of graduates waiting to enter the auditorium.

"There's Grandma!" one of my nieces shouted.

I turned and saw my mom in her black cap and gown. She looked as fresh and full of hope as a freshman. She stared straight ahead, poised for the future. I paused and took in her confident profile, then yelled her name. Mom flashed a winning smile and waved.

In the auditorium, we sat just two rows behind her graduating class. I watched as Mom giggled with her friends. They straightened one another's gowns and showed how to turn their tassel when it was time.

When Mom's turn came to walk across the stage, I jumped up and cheered. She smiled out into the crowd of faces. I blinked and I saw myself. I heard my mom hollering my name as I walked with my class through the Carrier Dome at Syracuse University. Even in that cavernous space, she reached me. I smiled up at the stands packed with people. I blinked again and saw my mom holding her degree.

After graduation, Mom thought we were just going to

dinner. But I had arranged a surprise party with friends and family gathered to salute her achievement. It was my turn to be there for her. She was the one holding the degree. But we both graduated that day.

Kelly Starling Lyons

Francie's Hair

Pick battles big enough to matter, small enough to win.

Jonathan Kozol

As my mother battled with me, as her mother battled with her, as her mother before her battled also (and that must have been an epic battle because my grandmother's hair was so long she could sit on it), I battle daily with my nine-year-old over brushing her hair.

This tug of tresses had ruined too many perfectly good mornings—leading to counter-pounding, tears at the bus stop, and a burning desire on my part to go into the kitchen and eat six or eight bagels with peanut butter.

There finally came the day that we asked Francie if she wanted to end it all. Wait! That sounds a bit dramatic. What we asked her was if she'd like to get her hair cut.

Short. Straight across, with bangs she could brush back on her own.

No more fights.

No more tangles.

No more tussles.

No more banging on the counter.

No more bagel remorse for Mom.

Francie was glad.

Dad was glad.

And I . . . was close to a meltdown.

If a psychologist were to examine this reaction (and that might not be a half-bad idea), the first thing the psychologist would certainly point out would be . . . this is not my hair. The psychologist would hear that we have always had in our family a freedom-of-hair policy. You can cut it; you can dye it (my eldest son once did, red, as in fire engine), you can shave it off. Hair comes and goes. We instituted this policy to avoid tattoos and body piercings, which don't come and go—or not as easily.

But as I tried to understand my feelings about Francie's hair, I realized I was in mourning. I was mourning because I have this bizarre notion that I own that hair. I love that hair. I cherish that hair. My daughter's luxuriant, long black hair, c'est moi.

It is so thick one's fingers can get lost in it. It shines like the hair of the landlord's black-eyed daughter. And I have an attachment to it that is unreasonable, so that even though I know it will grow back, I was having a terrible time parting with it even temporarily. I took time and reflected.

Self-esteem is not my best thing. I don't even like having my photo taken. Until we decided to have Francie's hair chopped off, I hadn't realized how much of my self-esteem was caught up with Francie's hair.

Why her hair?

I have seven children. Rob's wit, Danny's height, Will's smile, Mimi's lashes, Marty's singing voice, Atticus's baby smile: All these things, I realized, were things I regarded as achievements of my own. As if I'd had a part in them. They were like charms on a bracelet that I wore with pride. Thus, in the days before the haircut appointment, I suffered. I felt as though I'd had a diamond charm pulled off my bracelet.

I realized that this was an emotional issue, as they say. And I needed to get over it. I understood intellectually that this was nuts. But emotionally, I couldn't let go.

And neither could you if you had seen Francie's hair.

In our family, we have bad hair (mine and my younger daughter's), good hair (everyone else's), and Francie's hair.

Francie has the most magnificent hair, not just in our family, but within five miles. Within ten miles. It's like a river of patent leather.

People on the street want to stroke it. It falls in waves that movie stars spend hours in salon chairs trying to achieve before nights on the red carpet. People would kill for that hair.

But as a swimmer, a tomboy, a kid who would wear her Chatham Athletics T-shirt five times a week if we could keep it clean, she couldn't care less. She ties her hair up after she runs a brush through it, if she even bothers with the brush. Her long French braid is an ordeal to which she'll submit only for an occasion.

As we drove to the salon where her godmother would do the awful deed, I consoled myself. By the time Francie's hair grew back, she would be older, more responsible, more able to appreciate her hair the way I did. Happily, Francie could donate her hair to "Locks of Love," an organization that makes wigs for children who are undergoing chemotherapy treatment for cancer. You need at least ten inches of hair to spare to make a donation like that. I was proud of her, even as my brain nagged me with the knowledge that I was about to spend about five years without the irresistible joy of showing off, touching, and celebrating Francie's hair.

But the haircut would make Francie feel in charge. It would improve our relationship. She would no longer go to school, if she won the morning battle, with her hair put up in a careless ponytail and come home looking like a child in need of protective services, with hair so snarled it would have looked disgraceful on a squirrel.

And so when we got to the salon, we told our friend Stacey, "Go crazy."

The cape was fastened. Francie pointed out where she wanted her new cut to stop. I gulped. She'd pointed to her face at about the level of her cheekbones. Stacey got out the scissors.

And that was when Francie said, "Auntie, just trim the split ends."

I cried, "What?" But in all honesty, it was as if I were saying a novena.

Francie explained, "I get all this attention from grown-ups who say, 'You have the most beautiful hair in the world.' I kind of like that. I kind of hate the brushing (she shot me an evil look), but I guess I'm willing to put up with the brushing for the attention."

In the moment, I had regrets. I thought about the charity of Francie's choice and how it now would be denying a child who truly needed her hair—more than I needed her hair. I swear to you right here, I had not said one word to her about her choice. I said, in fact, "But you'll get attention for other things, for being strong and smart and good. . . ."

"This is easier, though," said Francie.

No fool she.

On the way home, I asked, "Do you want a milkshake?"

She asked, "Why? It's before dinner."

But I wanted to give her up an offering.

And you don't have to tell me. I know that I have to work on this.

Jacquelyn Mitchard

"Of course your mother embarrasses you.
That's what mothers are for."

My Critic

They say that time changes things, but you actually have to change them yourself.

Andy Warhol

I really had no idea how uncool and clueless I was until my daughter, Haley, turned twelve and I found myself living with my own private, personal, preteen critic. To think I'd lived all those years without realizing how unfunny my jokes are, how weird my taste in music is ("Mom, I don't care if you think Bob Dylan is one of the great poets of the twentieth century, the man can't sing!"), or what outdated taste I have in clothes and hairstyles. I no longer have to worry about leaving the house wearing anything the least bit "Maw Maw"or with my hair too "poofy." My twelve-year-old fashion consultant makes sure of that.

If there's spinach or lipstick on my teeth, I won't look in the mirror and wonder why no one told me. She'll tell me all right—with relish. Gone are the days when I'd leave the hairdresser's thinking, "I'm not sure about this haircut." There are few things less subtle than a twelve-year-old girl's eyes popping, mouth gaping, asking, "Mom, what did you do to your hair?" It's Haley's sworn duty as my preteen critic to make sure I know precisely how uncool, unfunny, and unsophisticated I really am.

Now, I've been accused of being an optimist, and I found myself wondering if maybe there isn't an upside to having at least one person in my life who'll be completely honest with me. After all, celebrities pay image consultants big bucks to do what Haley's willing to do for me for free. Take last month when I sang a solo at church. It was my first, and although I sounded great belting it out by myself in the car, when I got to rehearsal and took that microphone in my hand, my confidence wavered.

Aha, I thought, *Haley'll tell me the truth.* I'd committed to singing this solo and I wouldn't back out. But if I really sounded lousy, she'd tell me and I'd never do it again. As I dressed for work that morning, I was feeling pretty smug. I'd just call Haley into my dressing room and put it to her straight. *Honey, you're the one person who's completely honest with me. After I sing my solo Sunday, I want to know truthfully how I did. If you tell me I stank, I'll never sing another one. I promise.* This critic stuff isn't so bad, after all. I looked in the mirror and thought how much I liked the outfit I'd thrown together. It was slenderizing and stylish, yet comfortable. In fact, I felt like a million bucks.

I called Haley into the room and started my prepared speech, "Honey, you're the only person who's completely honest with me ..."

"Okay, Mom," she interrupted. "Lose the outfit!" She then turned and flounced from the room. I stood there with my mouth gaping open. *Where's that Bob Dylan CD?* I turned it up as loud as it'd go and felt a little better.

Then the phone rang. Ten minutes later, I called Haley back into my dressing room, fought back a grin, and told her, "Honey, that was Mrs. Shoultz. It seems she wants to put on a little play with your English class and was wondering if I could help out." Direct hit. There are few things more horrifying to a suddenly cool preteen than the thought of her mother set loose to parade her uncool, clueless self in front of her classmates.

"Mom, tell me you said no!"

I smiled!

"Please, Mom, you can't!"

The next day, I got dressed three times before Haley halfheartedly approved my outfit. "Isn't there anything else in your closet?"

All the way to school she drilled me, "No singing! No dancing! No corny jokes! Don't make up stupid nicknames for everybody! Don't tell any of your stories! Please, Mom, are you sure someone else can't do this?" I actually felt sorry for her as we stepped from the car and I had a flashback of my own dad dancing at my prom. But that was different. My dad was old and uncool.

I had a hard time locating Haley in the classroom as I started telling the kids about the play I'd selected. Finally, I recognized the top of her head buried beneath her arms in the last row. Then a funny thing happened. The kids started responding to me. They liked the play I'd selected, and clearly they liked me. I held myself back, and although I knew a couple of sidesplitting jokes that fit the occasion, I kept them to myself. When I caught myself skipping across the classroom, I stopped and maintained a dignified gait.

After ten minutes Haley's head came out of her arms, and as the other kids gathered round me for our initial run-through of the play, she joined in. At recess she shoved her way through the gaggle of girls who'd clustered to talk to me. She mentioned that the teachers' lounge was "That way" and that parents who help usually go in there but then settled down on the grass and joined in as we chatted. I did my best not to embarrass her.

That was last week. This morning as I opened the classroom door and the class let out a collective cheer, I think I saw Haley smile. She was the first to grab my arm at recess, and as we walked to the car at the end of the day, she said, "You know, Mom, I guess you're pretty cool for somebody your age."

"Oh, really? You think so?" I said as I reached for the car door, humming a Bob Dylan tune.

Mimi Greenwood Knight

A Perfect Fit

The natural flights of the human mind are not from pleasure to pleasure but from hope to hope.

Samuel Johnson

Clanging church bells broke the stillness of the hot and humid evening August 14, 1945. The ringing bells puzzled me, since it wasn't Sunday morning, it was Tuesday evening.

Before I could ask about the bells, Mom pulled me close and hugged me so tight it took my breath away. "The war is over! The war is over!" she shouted.

When I first heard about war I didn't know the meaning of the word. "Men are fighting far away across the seas so we can be free," Mom explained. At six, the explanation didn't make a lot of sense, but I knew no one liked war. But for me, the worst thing about the war was the rationing of shoes, and I didn't have shoes to wear for my first day of school.

I'd been barefoot and carefree all summer, but summer was coming to an end. Labor Day was only a few weeks away, and school would resume the day after Labor Day.

How I longed for a brand-new pair of shoes.

My feet became so dirty running barefoot all day long, every evening before I went to bed I had to scrub my feet with Lava soap to get them clean. That evening as Mom helped dry my feet, I asked, "Now that the war is over, can I have new shoes to wear on my first day of school?"

Mom frowned. I held back the tears; I knew what her answer was going to be. "Hon, you know we have to make do with what we have. Money is scarce. I'll try and fix your old worn-out pair. Come on, it's time for bed."

After Mom tucked me in and left the bedroom, I couldn't hold back the tears; I cried into my pillow so she wouldn't know how disappointed I was. I cried until there were no more tears. I couldn't sleep. I kept thinking about having to begin first grade wearing the uncomfortable, worn-out shoes hidden under my bed. And I envied my best friend Judy, who lived on a nearby farm; she'd be wearing a new pair of black patent leather Mary Jane shoes. How I yearned for new shoes, too.

It had been more than a year since Mom bought me a pair of brown leather shoes that were two sizes too big. The store clerk said we had to take what was available on the shelf. Every day Mom had to stuff my oversized shoes with newspaper so I wouldn't get blisters on my heels. Occasionally, my shoes would get wet, playing havoc with the newspaper stuffed inside. I was too embarrassed to remove the soggy newspaper, so I suffered until I got home. I'd run to Mom in my soggy shoes and apologize. "I'm sorry; I tried not to let the water get inside."

She comforted me the best she could. "Hopefully, one day I can buy you a new pair of shoes that fit your feet."

Each day it was more difficult to walk in the oversized shoes. When I ran and played, I tried not to smash down the back of the shoes. Eventually, the backs of the shoes were permanently damaged and unable to cover my heels. The lining inside of each shoe was rumpled, having dried that way after getting wet. This caused some discomfort as I walked, but wearing two pairs of socks helped cushion the irritation from the wrinkles in the lining. Mom tried to repair the old brown shoes by using pieces of gray cardboard to stiffen the backs of the shoes. I watched her carefully cut the cardboard to fit each shoe. She used a special needle and thread to attach the cardboard to the leather on the backs of each shoe. I watched her as she used a metal thimble to push the needle through the hard leather and the cardboard. She winced with each stitch she put into those shoes. "I'm so glad that summer will be here soon and you won't have to wear shoes," Mom said. And so was I.

The next morning I woke up early and heard Mom talking to Dad in the kitchen. Dad had been sick. He'd been diagnosed with a heart condition, and for the past year he hadn't been able to work the farm. There wasn't much money, and certainly not enough for new shoes. They were talking softly, so I got out of bed, tiptoed to the top of the stairs, and tried to eavesdrop on their conversation. Suddenly, I heard Mom's words loud and clear. . . .

Mom exclaimed, "I have an idea! The hens have been busy. Look at all the extra brown eggs I gathered this morning. I think we can do without a few eggs around here. I'm going to sell some to the creamery. People like to buy large brown eggs. Our little girl will have a new pair of shoes after all."

We all went to town that morning. Mom had no trouble selling two-dozen fresh large brown eggs to the owner of the creamery. And the brown eggs paid for a new pair of brown shoes for me. My right foot was measured for the perfect fit. Once the shoes were on my feet, I giggled and pranced in front of the special mirror for viewing one's shoes. Then I leaned over, gave Mom a hug, a kiss on the cheek, and whispered, "Thank you, thank you. I love them. Do I have to take them off?"

Mom hugged me back, "You can wear them home," she said.

Proudly, the day after Labor Day, I walked into the classroom wearing my brand-new brown leather shoes. They may not have sparkled as much as my best friend's new black patent leather shoes, but they were shiny enough for me.

Georgia A. Hubley

"I am NOT an antique. At 50 years old
I'm still considered a 'collectible.'"

The Mother I Never Knew

*When I stopped seeing my mother with the eyes
of a child, I saw the woman who helped me give
birth to myself.*

Nancy Friday

"I heard about this spa in the country," said my sister,
Joyce. "Let's take a long weekend and treat ourselves."

Joyce and I were in our mid-fifties, our kids grown and
on their own.

"Sounds fun," I replied.

"And let's ask Mom to come with us," Joyce continued.
"She never goes anywhere."

Our father had died years earlier, and our seventy-
eight-year-old mother rarely did much besides go to
church, the grocery store, and the beauty parlor. Still, I
didn't know if my frugal, no-nonsense mother would
enjoy a weekend of pampering. To my knowledge, she had
never even had a manicure.

I met Joyce over at Mom's, and she showed us the
brochure for our three-day getaway. Filling out the regis-
tration, I noticed the facility was touted as more of a health

farm than a spa retreat. But what did it matter? None of us had been to either sort of place before.

"That sure sounds like a lot of money," Mother commented. "The food better be good."

"The price includes massages and reflexology pedicures," said Joyce.

Mom shook her head. "I don't know."

"Since Mother's Day is coming, we'll pay your way," I replied, raising my eyebrows at my sister. She nodded in agreement.

"Well, I'm not letting anyone touch my feet, and I certainly don't think I'll take off my shirt and allow some stranger to rub on my body," Mom answered.

As I drove home, I wondered if Mom would enjoy herself. Growing up, there was enough money to pay bills and eat, but nothing extra for luxuries. We'd never taken a family vacation.

How would it be, spending all weekend together? We were close, but I didn't think of Mom as someone to have fun with. She wasn't like a friend . . . she was, well . . . my mother.

That Friday afternoon, we piled into Joyce's car for the four-hour trip to Oklahoma's Arbuckle Mountains. Our first activity at the retreat center was a mixer and welcome lecture. Joyce and I introduced ourselves to the other participants, but Mom hung back. I noticed she waited for someone to speak to her before she spoke. I never knew Mother was so shy.

Then we met Skye, the director. A hippy from the sixties, her long, straight grayish-brown hair was parted down the middle. Wearing a tie-dyed T-shirt, yoga pants, and Birkenstocks, she greeted the guests.

"Gather round." She motioned us to sit on pillows on the floor. I watched Mother as she slowly began to bend downward.

"Let me get you a chair." I started toward the dining room.

"No, Judy," she whispered. "I want to do what everyone else does. Just help me up when it's over." I never knew Mom didn't like to draw attention to herself.

The next morning, we walked down the hill for breakfast. The whole grain oatmeal was chock-full of nuts and berries.

"This is awful," Mom complained.

"It's only for a couple days," I said, trying to appease her.

"We should have snuck in some Pop-Tarts," Mom continued. "We could sell them to the others for a hefty price."

Joyce giggled and almost spit out her oatmeal. I never knew Mom had such a good sense of humor.

After breakfast, we took a two-mile hike. Mom was older than the rest of us, and at five feet two, her short legs didn't give her an advantage. Still, she tried to stay with the group.

"If you're getting tired, we can rest on that rock," I offered.

"Nonsense," she gasped between breaths. "I can do it."

We circled the grounds and went back to the lodge.

"Great going!" Skye patted Mom on the back. "You kept up with women half your age."

"I may be old, but I'm determined!" Mom winked. I never knew she was competitive.

Mother and I were scheduled for massages after lunch. "If you want, Joyce can take your place and you can rest in the cabin," I suggested.

"Why would I do that?"

"You said you didn't want a massage," I answered.

Mom was quiet for a moment. "Who knows? I might like it."

Not only did she get a massage, but Mom joined Joyce

and me in the hot tub that night. One of the other guests passed us as we walked back to our cabins.

"You don't miss a beat," she said, smiling at Mom. "I think it's great that you are here with your daughters. I wish my mom would do something like this with me."

Mom beamed. I never knew how much it meant to her to spend time with us.

As we snuggled in our twin beds, we giggled like girls at a slumber party. We laughed about Skye, the grains and grass we ate at meals, and our rustic cabin. It was nothing like the spa we'd envisioned, but we were having fun.

The conversation died down, and I pulled the covers to my neck. Mom seemed different here. I realized that out of the parental role, she could be a lot of fun. She was also shy, competitive, and proud—I'd never known that about her. For the first time, I saw her not just as my mother, but as a woman. And as a friend.

During the closing lecture, Skye encouraged us to let this weekend be a starting place for a healthier lifestyle. We said our good-byes. The first town out of the mountains, Mom pointed and said with a grin, "I see an ice cream shop. Anyone want a hot fudge sundae? I'm buying."

We laughed uproariously.

My healthy lifestyle didn't last long, but the new way I looked at my mother would last a lifetime.

Judy Spence

Ten Thousand Miles in Blue Streak

There are two ways of meeting difficulties: you alter the difficulties, or you alter yourself to meet them.

Phyllis Bottome

As a child raised by a single mother, my experience in the 1970s was different from that of my friends. I was a latchkey kid with more responsibilities than other children my age. But Mom worked hard, saved every penny, and made a comfortable life for us—one that included her passion for travel.

She purchased a 1973 Midas motor home and named it "Blue Streak." During a ten-year span, we traveled to forty-seven states. In my late teens, we pulled a horse trailer and competed in shows throughout Wisconsin and as far away as Ohio, Texas, and even Washington. I'll never forget the summer after I got my driver's license. We crossed the Continental Divide with me sitting in the driver's seat. I wondered how many sixteen-year-olds had ever done that.

Recently Mom was reminiscing about our earliest

travels. "Remember when we visited Graceland and toured Elvis's home?" she asked. "And wasn't it great overlooking Niagara Falls?" My blank response frustrated her—the only destinations I remembered before age ten were those she kept in photo scrapbooks.

"I took you to all those places and you don't remember a thing," she complained. I felt guilty—she was right. Then I contemplated my memory.

"No, Mom, I don't remember all the places we went," I said. "I don't recall this statue, or that museum, or even the lobster we ate in Maine.

"What I do remember, though, is that you were always there. It was just you and me for thousands of miles. I remember the orange shag carpet and the faded yellow curtains. I remember the RV water that smelled and the oven that didn't work because mice made a nest in the insulation. I remember reading the map for you and figuring out how many miles before the next rest stop.

"And I remember how you drove late into the night, while I fell asleep in the bunk above. You sang songs that started with each letter of the alphabet: 'Are You Lonesome Tonight,' 'Band of Gold,' 'Chances Are,' 'Don't be Cruel.' . . .

"I remember listening to your 'should have been famous' voice. That was my lullaby."

Now, over thirty years after my first trip with my mom, I've started traveling with my own daughter. I ask her to pick the destination, but she doesn't seem to care where we go.

"I just want us to go together," she says.

Where you're going doesn't matter as much as who's with you on the journey.

Kelly Curtis

Dancing with Mommy

The trick for grown-ups is to make the effort to recapture what we knew automatically as children.

Carol Lawrence

I hear the music coming from the CD player in the other room. At first, I'm prepared to yell, once again, to lower the volume on the boom box. But feeling particularly Mommie Dearest-like that evening, I decide that I will go down the hall to make a stronger impact and give the order in person. Like a tigress stalking her prey, I move slowly down the hallway. Sneaking a quick glance, I peer through the doorway. There, in T-shirt and panties, is my seven-year-old daughter, shaking her butt and singing the latest Pink tune. Something comes over me, and I turn and head back to my room.

My work clothes come off, and I put on my big white men's dress shirt a la Tom Cruise in *Risky Business*. Hair goes up into a ponytail on the top of my head. I pull out two hairbrushes, one for me, one for her. Slowly, I creep back down that hallway. The music is still blaring. I peek into her room again, and still she's lost in her moment and doesn't see me. Then I pounce. I throw open the door and jump into the room. She's startled, and I see the panic in her eyes. I couldn't make out whether it was because she thought she'd been caught doing something she shouldn't, ready to make excuses, or just embarrassed to be caught dancing around her room in her underwear.

My eyes beat down on her, mouth opens wide, and I raise one of the brushes toward my face, shake my own ample butt, and start singing . . . "'cause I'm a hazard to myself." She smiles. I hand her a brush and tell her to turn it up. I take her hand and dance her into the living room. And there, with the shades open, I dance like I'm Britney, Pink, and Christina all rolled into one, but for the audience outside my window, like a crazy, thirty-something-year-old exhibitionist.

I had a choice to make. I could go back to watching my TV, having my daughter lower the music and shut her door. Or I could choose to enjoy the moment that she was enjoying so much. I could be the disciplinarian and show her who's boss, or I could teach my daughter that even mommies need to let loose every now and then. It's good to be a mom with rules, but it's also good to be a mom who can bend the rules. Or maybe my choice was either to teach her or be taught.

For last night, I chose to take a different path than originally intended. And like so many other times in my life, I followed Robert Frost's words: I chose the path less traveled, and that has made all the difference.

Helene Kopel

4

TRIUMPHS LARGE AND SMALL

One way is not soft grass, it's a mountain path with lots of rocks. But it goes forward, forward, toward the sun.

Ruth Westheimer

Hurrah

I Am Ready

Health is worth more than learning.

Thomas Jefferson

There were many things I did not know about breast cancer. But equally important was what I did not know about myself. I thought I was strong, but I did not realize the strength I would need when I learned my daughter had a life-threatening disease. I thought I had lived through enough to prepare me for almost anything. I was not prepared for this.

Nor was I prepared for the guilt I felt because she was the one to suffer the illness, not I. Though I had my battle with uterine cancer ten years earlier, this was different. This was my forty-one-year-old daughter. The child I had protected. The child I would always protect.

It was not as simple as guarding her from the neighborhood bully when she was in grammar school. Or keeping her home in bed to protect her from a threatening cold. This was something much larger. Unexpected. Unfair. This was a sneak attack on both of us at the same time.

Other mothers' daughters got breast cancer. Not mine.

Other mothers' daughters had to face the treatment and the uncertainty and the fear. Not mine.

Only this time it was my daughter. For a while I thought I could handle my daughter's cancer. And I did. But then one night, as if my mind were playing tricks on me, it refused to listen to my instructions. When it was time to sleep, it would not. It was running full speed ahead, in a panic. And I was angry, so angry I wanted to throw things against the wall. I wanted to tell all my friends who did not have daughters with breast cancer not to pity me or my daughter. Not to look at us with sad expressions. Not to think it couldn't happen to them. Because it could.

The anger would not go away. It did not let me rest or eat. I did not believe other breast cancer survivors when they told me that one day this would fade into the past. Not then. Not at the beginning. Or that there would be days of joy returning. First, I had to run into the ocean with my daughter when she wore her new bathing suit with the prosthesis inside. Then I realized only she and I knew what she was fighting and what we were winning. I had to sing again at my grandchildren's birthday parties, and laugh again when the turkey burned at Thanksgiving as it usually did when I cooked it. I had to know I could run through the spring rain chasing a rainbow, and that my daughter would return to work and to life. I had to know we could talk about other things besides breast cancer, and that there would be days, weeks, and months when we would not even think about it. I had to know all this before I could help anyone else.

But now three years have passed. And I need to share what I have learned. I know somewhere today, this moment, another mother is getting the news that her daughter has breast cancer. And I know she will feel a part of herself shatter and think it will never mend. And I know she will ask herself, "How can this happen to me? To us?"—I want to tell her there is life after breast cancer. There is fulfillment after breast cancer. There is survival. I have so much to share with her—and I am ready.

Harriet May Savitz

The New Girl

It's never too late—in fiction or in life—to revise.

Nancy Thayer

I knew in advance that a new child would be entering my first grade class, and I dreaded the thought of having any new child come into this particular class, which seemed so antagonistic and competitive with one another. This class, more than any that I had ever taught, seemed to resent one another and the world. At lunch I heard over and over again "She got more than I did." "You let him go first twice and it was my turn to be first." I kept offering silent prayers to God: "Give me help, teach me how to change these children. Teach me how to teach them to love."

I arrived early and wrote on the board that we would have a new student coming into our class. Her name is Patty. I read this to the class and added, "Let's welcome her warmly." Then the questions came: *Where did she go to school before? Could she read? Did she like sports?* All important questions that a seven-year-old asks.

Then Patty walked in. She had bright red hair, freckles, an infectious grin, and a beatific aura about her. She stood in front of the class as I introduced the children one by one, and she had something to say to each one. She didn't seem to be thinking about who would be her friend or whom she would like. She just accepted each of us. The morning passed with no difficulties whatsoever. *The first day of its kind this year.*

Recess time came, and Patty was at the head of the line. Well, that was too much for Petey. He shouted that he should be first, and he started to push Patty. Patty just turned and said, "Oh, do you want to be first? I don't care. Take my place." The same thing happened at lunch over ice cream. Patty just gave the complainer some of her ice cream. The day flew by with bursts of generosity from this seven-year-old girl.

Near the end of school there was a rap on our door. I opened the door to see a dog with a halter-type leash leading a young woman into our class. Patty jumped up and said, "Oh, Mother, this is the best school I have ever been in." Then she turned to the class and introduced her mother, never mentioning that her mother was blind. The class was silent, and then the children in the front row stood up and went to shake Patty's mother's hand. Silently the class took turns, no pushing and no complaining.

Patty's mother thanked the class for welcoming her so warmly. Then she hugged her daughter and said to the class, "I hope you will all come to see us. We have so much fun together. Having a daughter is the best thing that has ever happened to me."

Then I knew that my prayers had been answered by the new child that had come into the room.

Julie Firman

Autumn

Look to your health; and if you have it, praise God and value it next to conscience; for health is the second blessing that we mortals are capable of, a blessing money can't buy.

Izaak Walton

Autumn, the season of transition, is upon us.

Children defensively zip up sweat jackets or button sweaters against the evening coolness, cheeks bright as candy apples as they play in the fading twilight, arrogantly unaware that winter's cold embrace is lurking. Older people nod knowingly and remember as summer's dog-day heat is replaced by the chilly relief of fall.

Even nature surrenders its colors to the season. The regal roses wither in the brisk breezes and are replaced by bold mums, their yellows and whites a last kiss of pigment in the garden. Along the streets the trees, forever reaching to touch the night sky, slowly lose their splendor, leaves turning brilliant and beautiful hues in a final good-bye before relinquishing their bough-homes and returning slowly, silently to the earth, leaving the trees themselves bareheaded and shivering in the winter winds.

It is October again. It has been a year since my mother has been diagnosed with inoperable lung cancer; a year since she embarked on her good, brave fight. It has been a year marked with so many milestones, so many shared smiles and secret fears. It was a year of recognizing blessings, usually passed over, and counting them one day, one hour at a time.

Children, with eyes that see all and minds that are still free to wonder, are extraordinarily accepting of the changes in routine, the shift in seasons. I know throughout her illness my mother's grandchildren have seen her change and have still recognized her always as "Mom Mom." This week, however, when I took my two younger boys with me for an impromptu visit to Mom's, Sean ran into her bedroom to greet her, then quickly returned to the living room to talk to me.

"Mom," my four-year-old whispered, careful not to be overheard or offending, "My grandmom has no hair."

Mom came through her exploratory surgery at Sloan Kettering and the radiation treatments that bombarded the tumor in her lung with faith, grace, and dignity. She also came through thin and tired—but without losing her hair.

This summer, however, Mom began losing something more precious to her—the ability to say words. Most of the time, she was able to hold a normal conversation (and normal in my family has always meant fast and furious). However, one day while talking to me, she had trouble saying the word Philadelphia. She knew exactly what she wanted to say; she just couldn't get her mouth around the sounds, and so she began spelling to me, "P-H-I-L-A-D," until I knew what she meant.

This began happening more and more often, usually when she felt weary or under stress, and by the end of August it was evident something was wrong. She returned to Underwood for further testing and learned that there were lesions on her brain. The pressure caused by the lesions was producing the speech problems. This pressure was dangerous because there is limited space in the skull for the brain to swell. Mom would once again have to go through radiation—this time quickly, intensively, and to the brain.

And the only side effect would be total hair loss. It should grow back eventually, but until it does my mother has a wig for her outings and scarves to wear around the house to cover her head. She wears these things mostly for the comfort of others. When she is alone, she usually leaves her head unadorned, finding the wig and the other accessories uncomfortable when unnecessary.

"My grandmom has no hair," Sean said, because we had caught her by surprise.

"I know, Sean. Isn't it funny?" I asked him as my mom joined us in the living room. We explained to him that Mom Mom had to take medicine that made her hair go away, but it would come back.

"Would you like to touch my head, Sean?" my mother asked as my son stared at her, his blue eyes filled with questions and curiosity. It is startling to see your mother—or anyone you love—without hair, but surprisingly it's something that you can get used to quickly. We are, after all, not really these bodies—these are just the shells that transport who we are, and no matter what the physical changes, those connected by love seem to be able to recognize their own. Mothers, good mothers, the ones who know that parenting is much more an art than a science, are a safety net for their children. They are the place we come to for love and acceptance, even when we feel lonely or unworthy or bad.

My mother has always been a personification of faith and caring to me, as well as a jumble of virtues and emotions and blessings as difficult to count as, well, the hairs on my head. One Tuesday recently, I sprawled with her on her bed, watching *Spin City* and chatting (which, thankfully, she does more easily since the treatments), when I asked her, "Is it cold, Mom? To have no hair?"

Each of us is born with many talents. Some of them are blatant—art and athletics, intelligence or beauty—while others are not as obvious, perhaps, but just as important. I have three siblings who each have a wonderfully nurturing instinct; they can see what needs to be done, the steps that need to be taken; they can define their roles and be counted on to follow through. I was the one who usually needed more direction, and I count upon their instincts and guidance more times than even they know. I consider it one of my greatest blessings to be their sister.

But one of my talents—one of those oddball ones that no one talks about—is that sometimes I come up with just the right question. "Is it cold, Mom?" I asked, and my mother looked at me and smiled.

"No, Mary, it's comfortable really," she said. Then with a sigh added, "It's funny, no one asked me about it before." We then talked about how she felt, how she preferred not wearing anything on her head, how hair loss was a small price to pay to regain *Philadelphia*. Once again I was her child, the role I knew best, listening to her as she talked of this, the newest challenge, the most evident change.

And then we were silent, side-by-side listening to the whispers of the autumn wind. I even fell asleep there, in my mother's bed, once again catching comfort where I knew it would be.

I can't tell you if I dreamt of the hope spring holds out to us that night. Perhaps not. But I do know that somewhere in that sleep I realized that there is beauty even in the barest winter.

Mary Dixon Lebeau

Beautiful

Nothing that is beautiful is easy, but everything is possible.

Mercedes De Acosta

It was a cold January day that found me struggling to pour a cup of coffee and adjust to having a brace around my neck after surgery. The sun shone, but the winds were harsh.

A few hours before, I'd been typing at the computer, poem after poem pouring from my heart. While at the keyboard a prayer came to mind, spilled onto the screen and down my face as tears. I tore the paper from the computer printer and placed my newborn prayer on top of the table amidst the many other poems stacking high.

The prayer was for my daughter and, for some unknown reason, my grandchildren "to be." Sadness filled my heart. My daughter no longer lived in our home. She had graduated from high school and moved out on her own to work and begin her own life. I missed her. While the relationship was not perfect, I loved her and wanted to share some moments talking and laughing.

A couple of days passed, when the doorbell rang. I gingerly but quickly went up the steps—to find my daughter standing there. It was good to have her visit. We talked, laughed, and the time spent was comfortable.

Photograph albums were piled beside her chair. I'd been working on them while recovering. The pictures that spilled all over the table made for even more fun moments as we relived the good times of her childhood. The conversation turned quiet, and her face clouded.

"Mom, my child will never have albums like these." She read my puzzled face quickly. She continued, "Mom, I'm pregnant."

Stunned silence filled the room as my head became dizzy. What does a mom do in this situation? Here, my beautiful eighteen-year-old daughter, once my baby, sat before me. Pain etched her face. Tears rolled down her cheeks, but I could barely see because of the tears falling from my own eyes. My mouth wouldn't work. I could not utter any sounds. My arms just wrapped around her heaving shoulders, and we sat a long time before either of us could talk.

Time stood still during those moments. There could be no judgment. She had enough of that for herself. This journey we'd travel together. There would be time later for problem solving and brainstorming ways to meet the challenges ahead.

Evening fell and I turned on a light as we began the road back to reality. Her eyes fell again on the pictures that surrounded her, and she spoke of her child with thoughtfulness. My mind's eye raced to the top of the computer desk. There must have been a shocked look on my face, for it seemed to alarm my daughter. "No, no . . . I'll be right back. Everything is okay."

Back in the room only moments later with a white sheet of typing paper filled with a prayer, I could barely speak.

"Here is proof that this baby is a blessing in our lives. This is a prayer I wrote two days ago—for your baby, and I didn't know why. It was just necessary to write it. I had no idea."

She realized I'd had no time to go type the prayer out in those quick minutes, and that it, indeed, had been written earlier. She read the prayer and once more we cried and hugged. She knew this was a confirmation that her baby was loved, that the child inside her was growing in purpose and was already being prayed over and cherished.

I wish it were possible to say the next months were easy. They were not. The one thing they were was wondrous. We shopped, planned, took pictures of her changing self, and experienced the ups and downs of motherhood together. She was beautiful. She changed from a little girl to a mom who loved her baby intensely. She blossomed into a responsible woman who studied baby books and attended classes on breast feeding.

The years have proved this young woman to be an energetic, creative, gentle, loving mom who is a strong advocate for her son and our most beloved grandson. We have spoken about the signpost in our lives—the typed prayer for her unborn son. It remains our own miracle of affirmation. It has a place in the continuing journal of his life. This daughter I love continues to be—beautiful.

Marilyn M. Ross

Christmas Blessings, from Grandma to Grandma

What is Christmas? It is tenderness for the past, courage for the present, hope for the future. It is a fervent wish that every cup may overflow with blessings rich and eternal, and that every path may lead to peace.

Agnes M. Pharo

While conducting Christmas programs at the Salvation Army's Women's Shelter, I was moved with compassion for the women and children living there. I met Margaret, a grandmother raising her two grandchildren. Margaret seemed much like me, except much older and recovering from a back injury, which left her unable to keep a permanent job. Margaret's daughter was no longer involved in her children's lives.

Sara, Margaret's granddaughter, was eleven years old. She was like most girls her age. She was excited about Christmas, but wondering if Santa was going to come to her home, which was now at the shelter. Billy, her grandson, was six years old. He was full of energy but seemed to be unconcerned or even aware of his surroundings. Sara was suffering the most from the loss of her mother, and though she was beloved by her grandmother, her world was much harder than carefree Billy's.

As I walked into the very small room that this small family called home, I could hardly hold back the tears. The room had two twin beds, which they shared, and they had to share a bathroom with another family. I listened as Margaret told me her sad story, shared her pain over her lost daughter, and finally showed me the one pair of shoes that Sara and Billy each had. She had no money to provide a Christmas for them. At an age when she should be cared for by her own daughter, Margaret's eyes became moist with tears as she thought about Christmas and how little she could do for her own grandchildren.

As a single working mother and grandmother, I knew firsthand of Margaret's most difficult and nearly impossible task. My heart was moved with compassion, and God began to speak to my heart about this dear family. It was through my own mother's words that I heard the message that moved my compassion into action. My dear mother used to always say, "There but by the grace of God go I." And for me, just one step removed from this sadness, I knew it was true.

I was limited in money myself, but I knew I had to do something. I sneaked a look at the shoe sizes Sara and Billy wore. I was on the move. First to the Family Dollar Store to buy toys and gifts. I loaded up! Then to the Payless Shoe Store, for not two, but three pairs of shoes; one pair each for Sara and Billy, and Margaret. Of course, there was the last purchase: wrapping paper and bows.

I hurried home and wrapped the gifts! I was so excited! I called the shelter and invited Margaret, Sara, and Billy to have Christmas lunch and to spend Christmas day in my home. Margaret cried tears of joy. I did not tell her about the gifts.

On Christmas morning, I drove to the women's shelter and picked them up. Anticipation mounted as I drew near to my home. Margaret, Sara, and Billy enjoyed a Christmas feast of smoked turkey and ham, chicken and dumplings, pecan pies, sweet potato casserole, and lots of goodies! Little Sara began to relax into the feeling of belonging that she had not had for so long. Billy just ate!

After lunch, we all gathered around the Christmas tree. I began to place each of their gifts at their feet. Margaret began to cry. Sara and Billy anxiously tore into their gifts! Sara and Billy had a new pair of tennis shoes and some toys. Margaret also had a pair of new shoes and a love gift of fifty dollars. There are no words to describe this scene. This was my gift. But whether it was a greater gift to them or to me, I can't say. I do know that this was the best Christmas I have ever had.

Carolyn Brooks

Mom, I'm Moving Out!

When we were children, we used to think that
when we were grown-up we would no longer be
vulnerable. But to grow up is to accept vulnera-
bility. . . . To be alive is to be vulnerable.

Madeleine L'Engle

"You and your daughter are so close," the salesclerk said as she led us to a fitting room. "You seem to have such a great relationship."

But a year ago, I wanted to say, *she wasn't speaking to me. I didn't know if she'd ever speak to me again.*

When I was hospitalized in 1989 for depression and health problems, ten-year-old Christy became the adult. She rose early each morning, made her older brother's lunch, and kept the household running. "My childhood ended when you went into the hospital," she told me years later.

After I came out of the hospital, I spent an hour a week in therapy groups, sorting out my childhood pain. It was a struggle to go home, be a parent, and function in the so-called normal world. Most of the time I slept. By Christy's seventeenth birthday, I felt strong. The therapy groups had ended, and my depression and health problems seemed over. Sure, our lives weren't perfect, but since the hospitalization, I'd worked hard to make up for my mistakes as a parent.

The memory of her previous birthday played back in my mind. Our relationship was strained, but I was determined to show her what a good mother I could be. I bought flowers and a cake. Balloons filled the family room.

In the past, she'd complained that I never bought her birthday cakes with funny themes, like the ones I bought her brother. This year would be different. I studied theme cakes in the bakery book and picked a cute purple dinosaur. She'll love it, I told myself.

After picking up the cake, I drove to my husband's office where she worked. *I'll surprise her,* I thought, *and she can share the cake with her friends in the office.*

Walking into the office, with flowers and a cake, I put the box in front of Christy. The other workers gathered round as she opened the lid. "Mom," she said with disgust, "this cake is for a three-year-old. You picked Barney! Do you know who he is?"

I had no idea.

"This is for little kids. How old do you think I am?"

"But I thought you wanted something funny—like I get for your brother," I said.

"Yeah, but not something you'd buy a three-year-old!"

I walked out of the office, carrying the flowers and cake. An hour later Christy came home, but we hardly spoke. When her dad came home, she handed us a letter:

Dear Mom and Dad,
I want you to know I'm moving out. . . . I don't want to hurt you, but I need a break from our family. . . . I

don't want you to know where I'm going. . . . I'll be in touch when I'm ready.

Love,
Christy

Was this some kind of joke? Minutes later a friend picked her up, and she walked out of our lives. We found out she'd been planning this move for months.

A few weeks later, Christy agreed to meet us for therapy, but only on her terms. Then the therapist invited my husband to join her in weekly sessions. I was not included.

My world shattered.

"They always come back," a friend at church said. Nothing comforted my broken heart.

Six months passed. *Was she hurting as much as I was?* I wondered.

Just before Christmas, my husband called from work. "Christy's been in a car accident," he said. "It's nothing serious, but she needs to move home. She'll need a ride to school and work."

At least she'll be home, I thought, knowing it would be difficult.

After weeks of being treated coldly, I approached her. "Christy, you've told everyone why you're angry with me, but you haven't told me. I need to know."

"I haven't told you because I don't want to hurt you," she said.

"Not knowing hurts me more. Please, talk to me."

Tears began flowing as years of pain, hurt, and disappointment poured from her heart. "You were never there for me when I was growing up," she said. "You were always sick or in bed."

I wanted to justify myself. *What do you mean I wasn't there for you? I was always there for you.*

Instead, I listened. I knew I hadn't been there for her emotionally. She had been the strong, self-sufficient child, the one who didn't need my attention. How grateful I had been for her independence.

Her voice interrupted my thoughts. "I felt like I had to raise myself."

When she finished, we sat in silence. Finally I said, "You're right. I was there for you physically, but I wasn't there for you emotionally. Everything you said is true. I'm sorry."

Her tears started again. "I know you did your best. I didn't want to hurt you."

I walked over and asked if I could hug her. As we stood embraced, I said, "It wasn't your job to take care of me. It was my job to take care of you. I was wrong."

"You don't know how hard it was for me to move out," she said. "But I had to do it."

"I admired your courage," I said and meant it. "And I respect you for sharing with me. You are right about your childhood. You did have to be the grown-up."

"You couldn't help it that you were sick," she said.

"That doesn't matter. I'm so sorry for hurting you. If and when you are ready, I hope you can forgive me."

I kissed her cheek.

Later that evening she said, "Mom, that's all I needed to hear from you. I just needed to know you understood."

Back in the fitting room, we giggled and laughed like old friends—no, like mother and daughter.

"You two are so close," the salesclerk said as she rang up our purchases. "You are so lucky."

Not lucky, I thought. *Blessed. Very blessed.*

Jeanne Pallos

"I'll have to admit I'm going to miss
the maternal goods and services."

Dancing Lessons

Happiness is not in the mere possession of money; it lies in the joy of achievement, in the thrill of creative effort.

Franklin D. Roosevelt

Six hundred anxious parents and relatives sat in the school auditorium waiting for the talent show to begin. Janice sat alone in the midst of the chattering crowd. It seemed everything she did lately, she did alone. Over the past several years her life had taken several shocking and unexpected downward spirals that had devastated her marriage and severely threatened her financial security. In the last few months her situation had only worsened, leaving her exhausted and hopeless. Now, despite months of fruitless searching, she was still jobless and even more stressed by her fast diminishing savings. She worried how she was going to provide a future for herself and her eight-year-old daughter, Renee.

Renee had one passion—to learn Irish dance. For several years, with a borrowed CD, she had taught herself a few steps and had even danced in front of both her first and second grade classes. This year, despite their situation, Janice had somehow managed to squeeze enough from her lean budget to pay for Irish dancing lessons. For four months Renee had practiced, determined to perform in this talent show.

She could not have been more excited or looked more beautiful than she did tonight in her borrowed Irish costume and shoes. Full of confidence, she was ready to dance! As the program moved through each performance, Janice wondered how her little third grade daughter would respond to this imposing crowd. In her short eight years, Renee had never faced such a challenge.

Finally it was Renee's turn. Janice held her breath as the curtain rose and the spotlight pierced through the darkness and onto her daughter looking so small and alone on the bare stage. The audience greeted her with polite applause and the music began.

Renee fell quickly into step with the upbeat Irish tune. Her bliss was evident as she danced and spun in circles around the stage. A few in the crowd began to clap with the music. More joined in until the entire audience, caught up in the irresistible beat, was clapping along with Renee as she danced lightly through her routine. Janice could not have hoped for a more affirming moment for her daughter. Then, the music ended and the audience began to applaud.

But wait! Janice wanted to shout. *What happened? The music shouldn't have stopped! The dance wasn't over!* Something had gone wrong but there was nothing she could do. Her daughter stood completely alone on that stage, her dance unfinished, with no one to give her direction.

While the audience continued to applaud, Renee glanced offstage, looking confused. Why had the sound man ended the music? She looked back at the smiling faces in the crowd and, in one quick instant, made a decision. With a grim look of sheer determination and with no music at all, she took her position and began to dance again. The audience, themselves now somewhat confused, grew quiet and watched.

In the silence of that auditorium, Renee danced on and on until she had finished every step, then looked straight into the audience and bowed deeply. Realizing what this little third grade girl had done, the audience stood and roared their approval with deafening applause, whistles, and loud shouts of *Bravo! Bravo!*

And Janice realized something at that moment—something her own daughter had just shown her. Though her own music had stopped, she must keep on dancing. She could keep on dancing! After all, if her daughter could do it, she could, too.

Armené Humber

An Oscar for the Warm-up

You are the architect of your personal experience.

Shirley MacLaine

My mother, seventy-eight, has been widowed for ten months. Although Dougie was her third husband, he was the love of her life. "Nighttime's the worst," she told me. "If it weren't for Jay Leno and *The Tonight Show* I don't know what I'd do."

My oldest son, Allan, now "in the business," surprised Mom with two reserved seats to the show. Mom was ecstatic and began counting the days. "I get to go on a Monday," she said. "That's when Jay does 'Headlines'!"

When the big day arrived, Mom stopped all liquids at ten AM "just in case" there might be "a need" during the show. "I don't want to have to use the restroom in the middle of the taping," she said. "I don't want to miss a thing!"

Fearful of heights and not as steady on her feet, Mom clung to the railing as we climbed the stairs to our seats in the audience. The "warm-up" for the show was already underway. Pop music performed by past *The Tonight Show* guests blared from suspended TVs while *The Tonight Show* crew prepared the stage.

"I can't believe I'm actually here," Mom said, gripping my arm with her long acrylic nails, painted French for summer. "Just being in any studio jazzes me up—the smell of the greasepaint, the roar of the crowd. Boy, do I love show business!"

No surprise. She's always said that not being a performer is the only regret she has in life.

A hip-looking forty-something man walked on the set carrying a duffle bag filled with what he called "presents" for the audience. "But only if you applaud loud," he teased us. His short bleached white hair stuck out all over and actually suited him.

"Mr. Warm-up" scanned the audience. "I'm looking for ten people to come down here onstage," he said as he began pulling individuals from the first few rows. A spotlight followed as he climbed the stairs to the higher rows.

When I saw him look at Mom, I knew he'd pick her. Her thick false eyelashes framed the excitement in her eyes. This man was searching for energy, and he had found it in my mother's expression. "You!" he said, pointing to her.

Mom leapt out of her seat (this, the woman who always asks me to "help me out of my chair"), leaving her glasses with the teenage boy seated at the end of our row. "I look better without the glasses," she told him. She descended the stairs, her fear of heights long forgotten.

The group was mixed—five beautiful young women, two middle-aged guys, an older woman (ninety), a man somewhere in his seventies, and my mother. Seated in the audience, I watched as Mom huddled with the group onstage getting instructions. They had been told that they were going to "dance for us." What if Mom falls? What if she slips? Can they tell that she's not steady on her feet?

The music was blaring. The stage was lit. The audience was in darkness, and I crossed my fingers.

The warm-up man called the first person up to the front of the stage on a small platform where Jay does the monologue. A tall dazzling beauty with a perfect body and long chestnut hair was great to look at, but she had no rhythm and was too self-conscious. The next beauty called to the front was even more mechanical. The third young woman was all about throwing her hair back and dipping low. The audience was responsive, applauding.

The rotund fiftyish man from Australia swung his hips like he had a hula hoop around his thick waist. More applause.

Next, the little ninety-year-old lady shuffled to the front, hands swaying and a wide smile on her face. Mom told me later that she had forgotten her hearing aid, so she had to "imagine the beat."

The audience adored her, clapping wildly.

A member of her family helped her offstage. There's no way Mom's going to get down to that platform, I thought.

Mom's turn. I held my breath. But my concern turned to excitement as soon as I saw her saunter up to the front of the stage, leading with her round hips. Effortlessly, she stepped down onto the stage platform and started dancing a little disco, a little rumba, it didn't matter. This was my mother's moment, and she was "in the groove." As she swayed her hips, snapped her fingers, and clapped her hands, the audience roared. They loved her.

The older man joined her on the stage. "Follow me," he mouthed to her as they bumped hips. The audience went wild.

When her time was up, Mom carefully stepped off the stage, clutching the little "present" the warm-up guy had given her. She climbed back up the stairs to our seats. Obviously, the adrenaline was propelling her the whole way.

The teenager handed back the glasses, and I hugged her tightly as Jay walked onstage.

"I did it, Heath," she whispered as Jay started the opening monologue. "For a couple minutes, I danced on Jay Leno's stage!" She showed me the present, a little stuffed monkey dressed in a miniature *The Tonight Show* T-shirt.

"This is my Oscar," she beamed.

Heather Haldeman

No Second Chances

*Let us not look back in anger or forward in fear,
but around in awareness.*

James Thurber

When I was ten years old, for reasons I wasn't told, my oldest sister and I were removed from the home of my parents and three other siblings and placed in a foster home. The first year we were allowed to visit our family occasionally for a few hours. Then the other siblings were taken as well. Two were adopted into permanent homes, and the last was placed into an orphanage, then later into a long-term foster home. We were told to forget about our parents and siblings, since we would never see them again.

It wasn't until I was eighteen that all the pieces of my origin came together and I was able to solve the puzzle I'd been piecing together since childhood. It was then that I was able to locate two of my long lost siblings and drove 2,000 miles to spend a few precious moments with each of them.

As fate would have it, I stopped for the night at an aunt's house, my mother's sister, who lived in Arizona at the time. I hadn't known my aunt well at all, but this was

a time for getting to know family, so when she invited me
to stay I figured . . . why not?

Aunt Bobby sat up half the night talking to me about
my mother. The mother I never really knew. I opened up
my heart to her and told her of my confusion, my feelings
of abandonment and rejection. I spoke of how I had both
loved and despised my mother but never understood any
of it.

"Your mother is what they call today 'mentally chal-
lenged,'" she told me. "She was the oldest of twins. Her
twin sister died at birth, and your mother was brain damaged to a slight degree. Doctors told our parents that she
would never progress past the age of twelve mentally,
though physically she would develop normally. Your
grandmother, our mother . . . well, she refused to accept it
at first. Then as time passed she had no choice but to learn
to deal with it."

Seeing my reaction to the information she'd just given
me, Aunt Bobby pulled me into an intense bear hug and
continued, "Though your grandmother tried to protect
her as best she could . . . she died at a young age and your
mother was on her own. She was used and abused
because of her mental capacity. She had three husbands
and gave birth to eight children . . . all taken from her.
Employers took advantage of her. She worked eighteen-
to twenty-hour days in a commercial laundry for less than
minimum wage. People mocked her and made fun of her.
She never drove a car, so she walked or took buses. Her
children were left at home unattended hours upon hours.
Still, with her limited capacity she nurtured each of you.
She loved you with everything she had to give; she gave
. . . all to no avail. Your dad was an alcoholic and seldom
held a job. He physically abused your mother and I'm told
he abused his children as well. That's why eventually the
authorities stepped in and placed all of you in protective

custody. In spite of all her efforts she lost her children."

I was stunned. This was the first time anyone had told me of this. Why not earlier when it might have made a difference? I might have been kinder, gentler with my mother had I only understood her. *Why didn't someone tell me long before now?* I was angry, and right on the heels of anger came a wave of almost debilitating sadness. Flashbacks sped through my memory like a slide show. Times I had shouted cruel things at my mother: "You're just stupid. Why aren't you like my friend's mother?" I remembered being embarrassed by the way Mother talked, the way she dressed. It embarrassed me that she could barely read or write legibly. I remembered not including her in mother-daughter functions because I didn't want my friends to see her. She took us to church every Sunday, but I did not want to sit with her in church. Stabs of gut-wrenching pain attacked me and I felt physically ill. I couldn't speak and could barely take the next breath the pain was so intense.

Aunt Bobby just held me and rocked me like a baby. Ever so slowly the pain subsided and I was able to think, to breathe, to sob. I sobbed for all the time I'd wasted blaming my mother for my misfortunes in life. I sobbed for all the hurts, sorrows, and disappointments my mother had endured. I sobbed for myself and my siblings who never knew the mother who loved us so much. I sobbed because I knew there were no second chances.

"I want you to understand this, if nothing else. Your mother loved you. Because of her handicap she has never held grudges. She was always able to see the good in everyone. Hurts, sorrows, and disappointments fell to the wayside, and only the good memories stayed with her. Who knows, if she'd had all the special care and programs they have today to help such people, everything might have been different for your mother. Still, she continued to live, love, and laugh because she knew she'd been blessed with eight blessings no one could ever really take from her," Aunt Bobby said as she stood to say good night.

A lot happened between the age of eighteen and today. I was reunited with all of my siblings and have grown close to each of them throughout our adult years. I've married and had three children of my own, thirteen grandchildren, and even fostered numerous others. Oh, yes, and did I mention that I was at my mother's bedside holding her hand when she took her last breath? I found my mother years ago and discovered, too, that God actually does give second chances.

Christine Smith

Higher Mathematics

There is so much to teach, and time goes so fast.

Erma Bombeck

My daughter doesn't know that she has a learning disability. She doesn't know because I never told her. I started to suspect that something was wrong when she was in sixth grade and still hadn't mastered the multiplication tables or even how to tell time. I met with her teacher, who told me that my daughter was a hard worker and a perfectionist. She was a child who wouldn't stop working on an assignment in class until she was satisfied that it was right.

But, the teacher continued, it took her much longer than the other children to finish her math worksheets. She had failed several quizzes, even though she was attentive in class and handed in all of her assignments on time. In turn, I told the teacher about the hours each night that my daughter spent on her math homework, about the frustration and the tears. I told her about the hours we had spent with flash cards, the time my husband spent with her every night helping her with her homework. Something was wrong, I told the teacher. I'm her mother, and I know. The teacher agreed to have her tested.

It wasn't a surprise when we met with the specialists after the testing was completed and they told us that she had a significant learning disability in math. In some ways it was a relief. It explained the lack of progress and enabled the specialists to recommend strategies and accommodations that would help her.

But I didn't tell my daughter.

At the age of twelve, she was already keenly aware that she was the worst math student in the class. The fact that she was a straight-A student in every other subject, a voracious reader, an outstanding writer, and had won the school spelling bee three years in a row made no difference to her. In her own eyes, she was stupid. I'm her mother, and I knew that learning this new fact would only confirm her negative self-image, and I was confident that the new strategies would help her.

So I didn't tell her that she had a disability.

By the end of the year, she was starting to do better. The school arranged for her to meet each day with a resource teacher who immediately reduced the number of homework problems that my daughter had to complete each night. She taught me some of the teaching strategies she was using, and gradually the nightly homework sessions became calmer. By the end of the school year, my daughter had a B in math.

My daughter is in high school now. Math is still hard for her, and by now she knows it always will be. She still says she is "bad at math," but she is also aware of what she has accomplished. She knows that if she doesn't give up, if she asks for and accepts help when she needs it, she'll do okay.

This year, she got an A in math, and she was thrilled. I was, too, but for a different reason. I know this A means that she has learned something far more important than just algebra and geometry. She has learned a higher truth, higher than mathematics—she has learned the absolute value of hard work, faith, perseverance, and confidence.

They told us when she was twelve that she had a disability; but I'm glad I never told her that. She then might have thought of herself as disabled. She might have thought that she had an excuse for doing poorly, or for not working as hard as she possibly could, or for giving up. She might have thought that she had a reason not to believe in herself; but she would have been wrong. I'm her mother. And I know.

Phyllis Nutkis

The Reluctant Rosebud

God gave us memory so that we might have roses in December.

James M. Barrie

Our town has a motto, which translates as "The Sea Enriches and the Rose Adorns." Every June, a pupil from the Senior School is crowned as "Rose Queen" and she serves for a year, visiting people in hospitals and helping raise money for charities. She has two assistant Rose Maidens and a group of ten little Rosebuds, who are her choir.

At eleven years old, the main goal in my life was to meet Elvis, and the last thing I wanted to be was a Rosebud! The chance to dress up in jeans and leathers and sing rock songs was my dream. It was not to stand on a platform in a frilly white frock with red roses in my hair singing Rabbie Burns's song "My Love Is Like a Red, Red Rose"! I knew if Elvis found out, he would never marry me!

I sang a lot to my mum, any song she liked, because that summer she wasn't feeling very well and had to spend long spells in bed. I went for the singing auditions, and I deliberately sang out of tune. My music teacher studied me, knowing that my voice was not the imitation of a strangled hen that I was producing. On the other hand, he had many other little girls keen to sing in the choir.

When I got home, I told my aunt I hadn't made it into the choir. My aunt studied me and asked, "Is that true? Did you actually turn up for the audition?"

"Of course I did," I protested. "But I don't mind; it's not important to me."

She sighed and said, "Sit down. I need to talk to you. Your mum and I have discussed this and decided you should be happy as long as possible. On the other hand, we just assumed you would get into the choir."

She looked uncomfortable, and I began to get a bad feeling about what she was going to say. "I am afraid your mum has a very serious illness. I am so sorry, but this time next year, your mum might not be here!"

I took in what she said and burst into tears. My mum, my warm, loving mum was going to die! I didn't just cry, I sobbed my heart out. I couldn't bear life without my mum. She and I were so close!

My aunt finally got me to stop crying so I could listen to her. "Your mum's greatest wish is to see you happy and to hear you sing. She is so proud of your voice. She has vowed that no matter how weak she may be that sometime, over the Rose Queen celebrations, she wants to see you up there singing."

I felt so bad that I had wrecked my mum's dream, I cried most of the night. They told mum I had a cold and had gone to bed early, so she couldn't see how upset I was. Just before nine AM the next morning, I was standing outside the music teacher's door. He looked at me in surprise, "Well, well, what are you doing here?" he asked.

"I did something really bad. I pretended I couldn't sing when you were doing the Rosebud auditions," I confessed.

"Yes, I am well aware of that, but I have plenty of other little girls who are happy to be Rosebuds. It's too late to change your mind now!" he informed me.

I looked up at him, and my voice was shaking as I choked out my plea, "Oh, please, let me sing. My mum is going to die, and she wants to see me sing in the choir. Please, help me!"

He was taken aback and took me inside and called my teacher. She already knew that my mum was ill. Later that day my music teacher told me, "Don't worry. You can go home and tell your mum you will be singing in the choir. No one will probably notice if we have eleven little Rosebuds instead of ten. Just let this be a lesson to you not to try to deceive people just to get your own way. God gives us gifts so that we can use them to give pleasure to others!"

I ran home, hugged my aunt, and went into mum's room. "I have to be out for a few evenings, Mum. I have to practice for the Rosebud choir!" I told her.

She clapped her hands in delight, "Oh, I knew they would choose you!"

On June fourteenth, after the crowning of the Rose Queen, we were ushered forward. I stood there with great pride in my little white dress, red roses in my hair, as we sang a few psalms first. My teacher then indicated to me to step forward as he announced, "Our lead singer will now start us off with 'My Love Is Like a Red, Red Rose.'"

He took me by surprise, but I sang out loud and clear. Mum was not the only one who burst into tears. Others were simply touched by the beauty of Rabbie Burns's words and music; Mum was bursting with pride at her little "Rosebud."

By that December, Mum was in a sanatorium and she died as the next year's roses were still in bud.

When I was fifteen years old, I was elected Rose Queen,

as they knew I was happy to go and sing for anyone at any time. The day I was crowned, I went along to Mum's grave and told her, "This is all because of you, Mum. I know you were with me today!" I put yet another bunch of red roses down gently on her grave. I was honored to be Rose Queen, but it wasn't nearly as important as it had finally been to be a little Rosebud.

Joyce Stark

5

LETTING GO

You must do the things you think you cannot do.

Eleanor Roosevelt

"I have to twinkle."

Leaving Home

As we move off into the future, two separate women each struggling to complete herself, I know that we will reach out to each other. In my strength I can be a tree for you to lean against. In my weakness, I will need your hand.

Rita Freedman

Before I got him, my husband bought peanut butter, mayonnaise, jam, cheese, and cereal in tiny, little boxes and tiny, little jars with tiny, little labels and tiny, little lids. As one who fed a thronging horde of voracious beasts, otherwise known as my children, several times a day, the groceries that I tucked into my pantry were stored in ultrajars and megaboxes, with jumbo labels and lids the size of a hula hoop. My husband lived in the Land of Cute Food, while I resided in the neighboring country of Super Foodstuffs, where peanut butter was purchased in twenty-pound pails. We still laugh about it, and on those days when everyone is out of sorts and getting on everyone else's nerves, one of my children will invariably remind my husband that he traded life in the Land of Cute Food for All of This.

I spent most of last week sorting through hope chests and closets, wrapping treasures in tissue and newspaper, packing boxes and making lists in preparation for the relocation of my eldest child to her very own home. This process forced the excavation of a lifetime's worth of cards, letters, toys, photographs, clothing, diaries, and so on. The exhumation of such ghostly articles was, in itself, traumatic. Coupled with the emotional roller-coaster ride associated with leaving home, the event was exhausting. They say the chemical composition of joyful tears differs from that of angry tears or tears of grief. They say every emotion imbues every tear with its own unique identity, and one who understood such things would be able to determine what the crier was feeling at the very second each tear was cried. Based on chemical analysis of our tears, I wonder how they would chart our emotional course over the last week—we experienced a shattering range of emotions, and we shed thousands of tears with each of them.

We laughed until we couldn't breathe at the fashions (is that what they were?) and hairstyles (a single ponytail tied above the right ear—what were we thinking?) captured in photographs of my child growing up during the eighties and nineties. Perhaps the tears we wiped away were as much tears of mirth as they were tears of relief that we had both survived leg warmers and headbands. Gifts bought but never given brought tears of heartache and betrayal. We wept in spite of ourselves amid peals of laughter at the memory of a Playschool Care Bear concert, and long-stored letters brought tears of sorrow at remembered losses.

My daughter's bedroom, the hallway, our dining room/front room/kitchen/back hall, the veranda—it was all a mess and we were a mess as well. Three days in a row, we cried our makeup into Alice Cooper faces, eventually tear-washing it off altogether. By the fourth day, we had decided not to bother with makeup at all, as any application to our swollen, puffy eyes would come off looking like some half-hearted Halloween effort.

There were protracted periods of indecision as my daughter agonized over which teapots to take with her and which to leave behind in the care of her mother. We discussed the relative merits of toothpastes and dish soaps and tinned milk. I explained (yet again) my smoke-and-mirrors approach to decorating, reminded her of my use-nothing-for-its-original-purpose theory, and showed her how to hang fabulous-looking curtains with thumbtacks and rubber bands.

Copies of *The Giving Tree* and *Where the Wild Things Are* were carefully stowed in boxes alongside cutlery and towels. We packed my daughter's down comforter, her featherbed, the trim green and blue bedding, . . . and her Strawberry Shortcake quilt. She took her Goldilocks and the Three Bears tea set but left her Bunnykins dishes so she would have something to eat her porridge from when she came home. The silver bomber jacket I wore in 1977 hangs forlornly in her closet, but the corduroy blazer I wore in 1980 was the first item into her suitcase. She packed pictures of her family but left pictures of herself.

Through it all, we wept.

In the last hours my daughter was at home, we sat around our dining table with her friends as I copied down the recipes she said she couldn't live without. As I wrote and listened and talked, I watched my daughter and remembered.

Before her, I wasn't a mother. Before her, I hadn't a clue how completely reasonable the idea of laying down my life for someone could be. Prior to loading the last of her worldly possessions for transport, I made a solo trip to the grocery store to gather a few supplies for the cupboards in the new apartment. I bought the smallest peanut butter, mayonnaise, jam, cheese, and cereal I could find, all of it in tiny, little boxes and tiny, little jars with tiny, little labels and tiny, little lids. Presenting it to her, I said, "Congratulations, honey, you are about to enter the Land of Cute Food." Through our tears, we laughed.

Done properly, the task of mothering, of parenting, ensures one sends a competent, confident, capable being forth into the world. For as long as I can remember (was there life before children? I seem to have quite forgotten), I have maintained that my job is to teach my children to leave me.

Have I done it all? I wonder. *Did I get it right? What did I forget? Have I told her about this, taught her how to do that?* And mostly, *Is it too late?*

Safely stored away in the Great Void, which is my basement, I have an embroidery pattern that features an entire garden of flowers and a single butterfly surrounding the verse, "There are two lasting gifts we can hope to give our children. One of these is roots, the other is wings." Watching my daughter leave home, I wept. I know I have given her roots and I know how strong they are; I can see it in everything she is. I believe I have given my daughter wings also, and I am fearful that they are just as strong as her roots. As she drove into the future, turning to wave tearfully back at me, I whispered, "Fly, baby. Fly."

M. Mylene English

First Day of School

It is my daughter's first day of school and I will not be there. Oh, I have been there for thirteen first days of school. Thirteen new pairs of sneakers, thirteen new backpacks filled with school supplies, thirteen kisses, and then a wave good-bye. Thirteen years of homework, permission slips, school plays, basketball games, parties, and enough other activities to wear down even the most dedicated mom.

However, this first day of school is different. This is my daughter's first day as a college freshman in a big city, no less. I do not know what she will be wearing today as she walks across campus to her first class, but I know it is not the denim jumper and pink T-shirt from kindergarten. I look at that picture from so long ago and wonder how thirteen years have passed so quickly.

She has traded in her pink Barbie backpack for a sturdy model in her new alma mater's colors complete with an extra pocket for her laptop computer, a hefty price tag, and a guaranteed lifetime warranty for extra measure.

I will not be checking her homework or proofreading English assignments. She does not need my signature on a permission slip or a ride to her best friend's house. I no longer function as her alarm clock or personal ATM. No more last minute requests for money for class photos, basketball shoes, or field trips. She will not be coming home after school today with conversation tidbits about who was wearing what, who is dating whom, which classes and teachers she likes (and dislikes), along with the regular complaints about homework and school food.

Today I watch the clock, wondering which class she is in right now, did she have time to eat lunch, is she making new friends? I realize that this first day of school is not much different from that first day of school thirteen years ago. Whether it is her first day of college, first day at a new job, first day as a new wife, or first day as a new mom, she is part of me and will always be in my daily thoughts. I will still worry if she is eating properly, if she has enough money in her wallet, and the big question, whether or not she still needs anything from me.

These questions just go along with being a mom. I did not sign on as her mom for just the first eighteen years of her life; I enlisted for all the years of my life.

Then she calls. I knew she would. She talks in quick, excited sentences. She likes the city. Classes are great. She likes all her professors. She has a lot of reading to do. Cafeteria food is good enough. She is meeting a lot of people and making new friends. By the way, she needed one more book and a new graphing calculator that cost $107. She charged them to my credit card. Is that okay?

I laugh to myself. What was I so worried about? She is my daughter and I am her mom. Despite the passing of years and the separation of miles, some things will never change.

Billie L. White

The Gray Slipper

*Shall we make a new rule of life from tonight:
always to try to be a little kinder than is necessary?*

James Barrie

"It's only a matter of time now," the doctors told me.
Mom was born in 1917 and her eighty-three-year-old
body was saying "Enough." I consoled myself, knowing
death would provide relief from pain and usher in a whole
new, wonderful experience.

Still, all I could think about was the gray slipper.

As the oldest daughter of five, and the only one who
lived in the same town as Mom, caretaking responsibilities
for the past ten years rested on my shoulders. Throughout
the course of this slow, debilitating process, Mom and I
had grown very close. Visiting doctors, finding support
care, moving her into various elder care homes as her condition worsened made for quality time, and sometimes
humorous episodes.

I still remember her first night at the convalescent
home. After tucking Mom in for the night, I left for home,
assuring her I'd be back to check on her in the morning. I

got a phone call that night from a nurse, complaining that my mother wasn't sharing the TV.

"What do you mean?" I asked.

"She says she wants to watch *Wheel of Fortune* and that's all there is to it. Her two other roommates want to watch something else."

Knowing that my mother is pretty much incapable of getting in and out of bed by herself, I asked the obvious. "Why don't you just turn the channel?"

"She doesn't want us to!" the nurse exclaimed.

I laughed inside. Mom always had a way of controlling a situation. I knew the same obstinacy, exhibited in her personal opinions, had allowed her to live so long, in spite of bad health. Maybe that's why seeing her in the hospital now, so docile and weak, was taxing to my soul.

It was only two weeks ago that my mother had been admitted to the hospital for what they believed was a cracked hip. The x-rays proved negative, so she was released and sent back to the convalescent home. That night the hospital called me to report that my mom had left behind one gray slipper. Knowing I had just purchased a new pair for her, and realizing she was probably through traipsing the halls anyway, I instructed them to throw it out. While visiting my mom at the convalescent home that night, I told her about the stray slipper.

"I love those slippers; they are so cozy," she whined.

"I already told them to throw it out. Besides, you have this nice new pair," I assured her.

"Go get the other one, please," Mom begged.

"I can't. It's late. I'm tired, and it's probably already on the bottom of the trash bin."

I left that night feeling a tinge of guilt, but at the same time justified in my resolve.

Tonight, however, standing beside her hospital bed again, guilt gives way to remorse. I know people often live with regrets, good-byes left unsaid, deeds left undone, but I was determined I would not endure such a fate. Now I wished for another chance to say "I care."

I care enough to give you hope, for a slipper you would never wear, to give you comfort in familiar things, to give you a feeling of worth, dignity, and control when all around you seems helpless and your personhood stripped. I knew if given the chance again, I would not betray a trust.

The hours ticked away and Mom drifted in and out of sleep. My stomach growled. I kissed her cheek and slipped away for a quick bite. My sister arrived, agreeing to keep vigil. As I sat alone in the cafeteria with my contrite conscience, I couldn't help but wonder about the people dining around me. Do they know how precious life is? That each day is a gift from God? Do they realize the opportunity they have to touch another life tenderly, leaving what might be their last impression?

I knew my mother would forgive me for the lost slipper; we had too much good history together. Still, I felt a shadow of regret that I acted so hastily. I finished the last of my coffee and headed back up to the room. When I walked back in, Mom was awake. She looked happy to see me.

"Oh, look," my sister said. "A policeman came in and made me sign for this. He said it belongs to Mom." I blinked in utter disbelief. It was the gray slipper.

"I don't care who you think brought that in," I told my sister, "an angel sent this to me."

"A slipper?" my sister asked. "Mom can't even walk. She doesn't need it."

"It's not for her," I said, holding it to my chest. "It's for me."

Pearl Nelson
as told to Lynne M. Thompson

[AUTHOR'S NOTE: *Alberta Anderson passed away on July 2, 2000. The gray slippers remain in Pearl's closet to this day*].

Dancing with Mom

Mother had been gone for over ten years, but I still wondered if I'd ever feel peaceful about the way things ended up between us. I like to think of myself as a kind and loving person, but I made some big mistakes with Mom. I realized that God works through all people and situations, no exceptions; but when it came to Mother, I often felt unworthy of receiving a release. The truth is I felt guilty because I didn't know how to love her well enough during her prolonged illness.

Lately I've been cleaning out my basement in anticipation of moving to a new place. My basement is the repository of Mother's things and relics from my childhood. Touching her books, magazines, and handwritten recipe cards helps me to remember her before she got so sick. When I unpacked Mom's English Spode china, I flashed back to helping her set the table for company. She trusted me to handle the plates when I could barely see over the top of the table! The feel of the plates in my hands, reminded me of Mom's faith in me. Her trust seemed well-placed in those early years. But did I let her down in the later years? The dishes were a good starting point; they connected me with happier times with Mom.

I also found my rag doll, Susie, the one with yellow yarn hair and a big smile. Susie was my imaginary best friend when I was a girl. I began to dance with Susie, like I used to when I was little. Good memories wafted over me like a refreshing breeze blowing through a window stuck shut for too long and finally pried open. When I was three, Mom patiently taught me how to load records onto the turntable. As long as I was careful putting the needle down on the vinyl, I was allowed to play any music my parents had in their collection. Mom and I would dance to tango music and eat squares of chocolate with almonds. She introduced me to the music of Beethoven, still my all-time favorite composer. Also, Mom was quite a musician in her own right. She sang and played the piano beauti-fully. Her favorite piano solo was called "Nola." It was exu-berantly joyful, with thrilling runs and bouncing rhythms. I would dance to the music as she played—leaping and pirouetting over and around the furniture.

I was a very wanted and loved child. Mother didn't have me until she was thirty-eight. She had lost a baby before I was born, but she was determined to have another child. I was born without a hitch. Mom was fiercely determined to see me thrive. She knew what my spirit loved! Not all children are so blessed. Actually, as I remember back to my girlhood, Mother was my real best friend.

Mom started having serious health problems when I was fourteen. She'd had six major operations by the time I was twenty-two. In my teenage years I'd play the piano, and Mother would listen, sitting in her favorite chair. One of the saddest times came in my early twenties. She went through excessive radiation treatments to make sure that a small spot of cancer had not metastasized. The treat-ments pretty much wrecked her lower intestine. She was flown by private plane to the Mayo Clinic, where a team of surgeons miraculously got her plumbing to work again. Although I was a bride of only four months, I flew in to stay with her until she could go home.

Nine years later, just weeks after the birth of my third child, I was listening to a record of Beethoven's seventh symphony when the phone rang. It was Mom. She sounded like she was talking with a mouthful of marbles! I had no idea what was going on until my dad got on the phone and told me she'd had three seizures and probably a little stroke that week. Part of me wanted to hop on the next plane so I could be with her. But I was a mother now, and my first loyalty went to my newborn son, my two young daughters, and my husband. Dad would just have to deal with things on his own.

I always figured Dad would outlive Mom. He'd always been the strong, healthy one. Who can ever figure? He died when my baby son was two.

Mom lived another eleven years. She couldn't live alone. I found a lovely retirement home for her a few miles from my home. She had a large private corner room and plenty of care. She made an amazing adjustment! Her health rallied long enough to fall in love and remarry! She was seventy-five and he was ninety-seven. They lived together blissfully for two years. Then Mom started to have seizures and strokes again. Her dementia became more severe.

This point is the part of the story where I usually get bogged down. Maybe some daughters know what to do when their moms are no longer able to do the most basic things. Maybe I should be grateful that I had a mother's love to receive as long as I did. But I'm angry she got so sick. I also feel guilty that I didn't invite Mother and her husband to live with me. Sure, we might have all gone bonkers together, but she hated the nursing home. She would phone to tell me that she was going to walk out and that I should come pick her up. I visited her when I could. Her husband drove over to see her almost daily. I feel guilty I didn't visit her more often. I feel sad that she was lonely. I feel awful thinking that she might have been scared. The problem with all these feelings is that they connect me only to the suffering—and to my negative self-judgment. My guilt blocks access to all the best parts of what I treasure about Mom. I think she'd want me to remember better times.

Coming from the basement, done with another day's packing, another day's memories, I look in the mirror and I notice that the set of my jaw, my eyes, and the way I smile look just like her. She's communicating with me. I stop and listen to her message. I can hear her saying, "Remember me in my health! Remember me as your young mother. I'm there with you in all those happy memories." A little guilt still arises, and I listen a little more intently. "Mistakes happen—yours and mine. I forgave you for being so busy a long time ago. It's time to forgive yourself. Let go of the guilt."

Glancing at the mirror, I can see I have relaxed; my face is softer, my jaw less tight, my mouth turned up in just a tiny smile. I turn to get on with my still-busy life, and I hear her last words, the ones I will carry in my heart from now on, "If I could tell you just one thing, sweetheart, it's this: Love is the important thing and love never dies. And remember, honey, there is always music for dancing."

Sally Singingtree

Empty Room, Empty Nest

Where we love is home, home that our feet may leave, but not our hearts.

Oliver Wendell Holmes

I gazed around my daughter's bedroom; the baby quilt her grandma made, the silver-framed pictures of her high school buddies, the bulletin board with the bright red university pennant. Suddenly it dawned on me. *This bedroom may never be Kate's real home again.* It didn't seem possible my little girl was almost ready to graduate from college and go off on her own.

As I was rummaging, my husband, Mike, peeked in the door. "What are you doing?"

"Just looking." I moved aimlessly, touching the soft pillows on the neatly made bed. I was happy Kate was off pursuing her dreams, but of course I still missed her terribly. "I can't get used to this room being empty."

"Remember when it was so full of toys and books and stuffed animals there was practically no room for Kate?"

"Wasn't that just yesterday?" I laughed. It seemed she was just a little girl dressed in pink, carrying around her redheaded Cabbage Patch doll. From the time we taught her to walk, to the hours teaching her to drive, I never thought we were actually preparing her to . . . well, leave.

I picked up the hand-knit booties she had kept all these years, now a dusty decoration. Had her feet really ever been this tiny? Twenty years ago, we'd started a family. Now our little girl was off and on her own. But I wasn't ready!

As Kate grew up, the room had gone through many transitions: from the charming teddy bear wallpaper, to the big girl, frilly pink bedspread and curtains, to the updated blue comforter and sophisticated framed prints on the wall. Mike and I guided Kate through the first day of school, first date, and first heartbreak. All those times teaching her right from wrong, through laughter, tears, and hugs, only for her to grow up and leave. Of course, that's why we did it. But now, the room was vacant.

I started to leave, but noticed the dresser drawer ajar and moved to close it. Inside, I spied a few bottles of nail polish, a silk scarf. "Look, here are her warm socks. I told her she'd need them, but she never liked the way they looked."

"Kids," Mike scoffed gently. "They always manage to leave something behind."

Those words turned over and over in my heart. And then I knew my husband was exactly right. Kate had left something behind. But it was not scarves and socks; it was a part of her. And it would stay with me no matter how far away she roamed. I may not see her every day at the breakfast table, or wait up every night for her car to pull in the driveway. But the fun memories of times together and the stories of her new independent experiences surrounded me every day. Yes, things had changed. But I could always feel my daughter with me, even when she was far away.

I took one last look around and walked out the door. Maybe it was time for that bedroom to undergo another transformation—an office, or an exercise room? Or maybe for now I'd leave it just the way it was, with Grandma's quilt and the framed pictures. Kate may have grown up and flown the nest, but I knew she'd always come back and visit. And I'd always have the part she left behind.

Margaret S. Frezon

Poems for a Daughter, Gone

1978
Lisa—my darling dancing daughter,
glinting smile, mischief in your glance,
firstborn child, full of beauty,
lighting up our lives
with love and dance.
Little magpie
chattering the livelong day,
sharing all your world with everyone—
flitting here and there
from room to room,
never still for long
and seldom quiet.
Six years old and suddenly
so grown-up,
reading words that
yesterday were strange;
knowing all the answers
to your questions
and yet so innocent
and (somehow) touching.

Stay, my little Lisa,
stay awhile,
don't grow up so fast—
don't go away.
(And on she sleeps, her
teddy tucked beneath her chin,
eyes and mouth closed sweetly
vulnerable.)
I love you.

1984
Fourteen years since
you were born,
years of trial,
years of joy.
Fourteen years—
almost a woman.
(Yet still, a moment
for your toys!)
Fourteen years since
you were born,
but with assurance
we can say:
Fourteen years,
almost a woman,
but loved as much
as that first day.

1993
When the door opened, my world rocked on its axis.
The uniforms said my daughter, my firstborn, was dead.
Gone.
Time stood still as I absorbed the scream inside,
then rushed by as I went to tell my world.
Gone.

Her damaged body was put into the earth unseen.
My empty arms ached to hold her just once more.
Gone.
The shock wore off as the pain wore on and on,
but God's song filled the hole his call to her had left.
Gone.
Someday, I'll hear his voice calling me.
I'll leave this place of sorrow and I'll join them.
Gone.

1993
Some future distant day, we will hold out our hands
to others who are drowning in their grief.
Someday, we'll share the wonder of God's love with them,
the surety of faith, and sorrow's end, the start of hope.
But now, today, we got up, dressed, and went to work.
Today . . . today, we didn't cry. It was enough.

1994
The Things She Left
A coffee mug with reindeer,
a flowered plate from camp,
an afghan from her grandma,
a broken hob-nailed lamp,
A doll she named "Bianca"
and a pair of old camp mocs,
two T-shirts that say "Lisa"
and an inlaid wooden box,
A tape of gospel music,
three earrings without backs,
a sleeping bag, some textbooks,
and a box of dental wax,
The pieces of her daddy's heart,
her little sister's tears,
her brothers' grief, her mother's pain,
and a lot of unlived years.

1998
She flew through life
and lit up every space
with sparkling smile
and dance of joy and grace;
then left us to go
light another place
and dance her dance
before God's very face.

Betty Winslow

That's What Mothers Do

What the daughter does, the mother did.

Jewish Proverb

Nineteen fifty-eight was a busy year for Evelyn Hill. At thirty-eight years of age she gave birth to a healthy baby girl weighing in at nine pounds twelve ounces. She brought me home from the hospital, arriving almost simultaneously with my maternal grandmother, who was moving in to be cared for during her final months. Dad was the pastor of a small church, my eleven-year-old sister helped whenever she could, and Mom held everything together with her calm demeanor and steady hands. My early days were not spent in a crib, but cradled in the arms of my grandmother so that my mother could take care of both of us at once. That's what mothers do.

Nineteen eighty-five was another busy year. This one for me. I had just gotten married in December and was in my first year of graduate school. My new husband was a corporate sales manager, and our days were filled with work, school, church, family, and friends. In July we found out that I was expecting a baby. Three weeks later, I kissed my husband good-bye as he left for a three-day business trip. Patting my tummy he said, "I miss you both already."

That Friday, August 2, 1985, was hot and smoggy, and I dressed carefully in a light yellow shirt and navy slacks to look nice for picking up my husband at the airport and for the party we were to attend that night. When I received the news that his plane was delayed, I asked the ticket agent how long the delay would be. She quietly responded, "We have no estimate of time of arrival." I thought it was an odd response but soon learned the reason why. There had been a plane crash and my husband of seven months was a passenger. There were a few survivors, but the odds were not good.

My parents were there very quickly, and Mom kept uttering the words, "It can't be true, it can't be true, can it?" It was. The phone call we were dreading came at four AM, and my mother held my hand as I heard the airline representative say the words, "It is my sad duty to inform you that your husband did not survive the crash." Dad took the phone while Mom just held me close. That's what mothers do.

During that next week, I would wake up crying each morning and she would comfort me, pray for me, and care for me. Her days were spent making me any food that I remotely thought I could keep down, a short list at eight weeks pregnant. She also served as my filter from the real world. She understood, without asking, that there were only certain people I wanted to be with or even talk to, and she kept the others away until I was ready.

Even though Mom was totally inept with a curling iron, she attempted to curl my hair for the funeral. We both ended up giggling so hard that my niece had to take over. Being able to laugh with her released the tension of that difficult day. Mom was also with me when I walked back into our home and immediately scooped up his favorite sweater, just to hold and smell. Although I knew her heart was also breaking, both at the loss of a much-loved son-in-law and at watching me in pain, she was always strong for me. No amount of snapping at her in frustration or angry tears could shake her loving care and tender words that first awful week, or anytime after. That's what mothers do.

Seven months later, a healthy baby girl was born, and Mom and Dad were there to drive us home from the hospital. Mom taught me to care for her and was always available with good advice. Now age sixty-six, she drove forty-five minutes one night a week and spent the night on the couch with Katie sleeping next to her so that I could have a really good night's rest.

When Katie was four, she came into the kitchen one afternoon and announced that she was having a "really bad day."

"Call Grandma," I told her. "She makes me feel better when I'm feeling sad." I dialed and she curled up in the chair, twirling the phone cord in her toes, to tell Grandma all about her bad day. When she was finished, she hung up with a smile and went back to playing.

During Mom's final years, arthritis slowed her down, and my phone would often ring midmorning. It would be Mom saying, "I just missed a phone call. Were you trying to call?" I would know then that she was having a really bad day and needed to hear my voice. After chatting for awhile I would always hang up with a smile.

Right before she died, I spent a few nights with Mom so that Dad could get a good night's sleep. As I cared for her through the night, we held hands, prayed, laughed, cried, and talked about the times we had shared. For I have been well taught. That's what daughters do.

Cheryl Riggs

Rite of Passage

Because I have loved life, I shall have no sorrow to die.

Amelia Burr

The quilt fit perfectly on the bed in front of me. I studied the blue and white cover, made by our family, as I tucked in the corners. The squares represented aspects of her life, each one a motif of an activity, a hobby, an honor, or a relative—reminders of people who loved her, now that she was far from home.

"Looks great, doesn't it?" I asked her.

"Why, yes, it does," she replied quietly, sitting in a chair watching me.

One of her new roommates was asleep, so we were trying not to make a lot of noise. The room was a triple, and the third bed was as yet unoccupied. I wiped a bead of sweat off my face.

"Hot, isn't it," I said, stating rather than querying.

"Mmm," she murmured.

I wonder who's more nervous about parting—her or me? I sighed, reconciling myself with the knowledge that she was entering a new phase of her life, and she was letting me help usher it in. I would unpack her suitcase and place her belongings around her new abode. Then, when I left, she would put them wherever she wanted. Typical mother-daughter interaction. *Must be wired in our DNA,* I thought. I could smell lunch cooking in the kitchen down the hall, reminding me of the time. I kept myself calm by the orderly placement of clothes marked with her name in black laundry pen.

"Shall we put this family photo by your bedside?" I asked her.

"Oh, that would be nice," she smiled, pulling at a thread in her sleeve.

I wondered what she was thinking about. Should I worry because she's just sitting there?

"When are you leaving?" she asked.

I looked at my watch.

"Soon," I said, lowering my voice when her roommate began stirring.

The door by the empty bed was open. I peeked in.

"Look," I exclaimed. "You three will share a bathroom. It's pretty large."

I took in her hairbrush, toothbrush, and plastic cup, each of which I had marked with her name: TONI. Almost like going to Girl Scout Camp.

Finally, there was nothing left to hang, spread, lay out, tuck in, or unpack.

"Honey," I said, with just a trifle of a catch in my voice, "I know you'll do well. I'm so proud of you. I love you more than words can say."

"Me, too," she replied, turning her blue eyes—the same shade as mine—directly toward me. I hugged her tightly, not wanting to take my arms from around her small body.

"And I'll come see you soon," I reassured.

She nodded, not meeting my eyes any longer.

"So I'll be going now," I added, straightening the teddy bear on her bed.

She was looking around the room, soaking it all in—her new life. Soon she would meet the gals down the hall in the dining room.

"Don't take any wooden nickels," I called, blowing her a kiss as I opened the door. That brought a smile. I closed the door behind me and walked down the hallway, past other doors with beds and dressers and desks. The sunshine felt hot as I walked toward my car. Tears held back for so long were now dripping off my chin. As I wiped them away with the sleeve of my green sweater, I tried to figure it out. Which could be harder: leaving your oldest daughter in her first college dorm room, as I would do in a few years, or leaving your mother in her first assisted living facility, as I had just done?

For I was the peanut butter in the Sandwich Generation, holding together the lives of women on both sides who meant the world to me.

I started the car, driving away in the blue minivan our three young daughters had dubbed the Sardine Can. Time to pick the younger two up at school . . . time for ballet and basketball practice. My chin was quivering like crazy.

She'll be fine, I told myself, wondering if I would be.

And she was fine. She lived in that small personal care home for ten years with Alzheimer's, whom I called "Al." She made new friends—over and over and over again. She was as happy as she could be anywhere. We visited her often. The family who ran the home became like extended relatives.

And yet, how odd it always felt to introduce myself to the woman who had brought me into this world. But those were Big Al's terms.

The night my mother died, our eldest daughter drove three hours from her college dorm room to share that special time, arriving at midnight. We massaged her grandmother's limbs with scented lotion, telling her how much she meant to us.

There we were together, three generations of strong women, two of us helping the third move gently into still another new home.

Lanie Tankard

Caring for Mom

It's been three weeks since my eighty-two-year-old mother fell. Although she didn't break anything, she is badly bruised both physically and emotionally. Her already small world has now turned smaller as her fear of falling again keeps her homebound.

This is not the first time she fell. She's fallen twice in the last two weeks. Her podiatrist told her to stay off her feet in order to let an ulcer between her toes heal. Instead of exercising in a chair, she took him literally and has spent most of her time reading or watching television. The more she lay around, the weaker she became. Now, far weaker than she has ever been, she mourns the woman she once was and wonders what will become of her.

"You're weak because you haven't used your legs." I tell her. "You need to move, walk, and exercise."

My mother, who throughout her life has only equated exercise with shopping, will have no part of my reasoning. Besides, she's heard all of my preaching before and has learned to tune me out.

"Aimee, I'm not feeling well. You don't understand. I'm all black and blue," she tells me in an irritated tone.

"You've fallen worse in your life than this time." I say to

her. "You've always gotten up and moved on. Get up now, get dressed, and let's go grocery shopping together."

For a moment, the silence between us feels unusually heavy.

"You're right," she says as if a light bulb has lit up in her head. "I'll get dressed now. "

An hour later we are in the supermarket. Her walker has been replaced by a grocery cart, which she clings to for support. Slowly down the first aisle we go. It has taken me years to learn to match her pace. I'm so used to the speed dance of the business world that anything slower feels like I am moving through molasses. Patience has never been my strong suit, but after realizing the stressful effect my pace has on her, I have trained myself to take baby steps to match hers. Even so, at times I forget, and she needs to remind me.

Rounding the corner into the second aisle, my mother begins to moan. As walking is clearly difficult for her, I suggest I get some items from her list. Racing down the aisle to find her French vanilla coffee, I see a woman my age— fabulously fifty—with her elderly mother. But instead of looking dynamic, this attractive woman looks uptight and frazzled. As I stop to find the coffee, I overhear her talking to her mother in monotones that reek of annoyance.

Compassion, I think to myself. *This woman definitely needs to find her compassion.*

For the next five minutes I walk up and down the aisles finding my mom's items and putting them into her cart. By now, my mother's moaning has gotten louder and in hearing it over and over again, I become agitated and annoyed. Internally I am struggling between concern for my mother, whom I love dearly, and suspicion that she is manipulating me by playing the drama queen. As I enter the frozen food aisle to get the last item, I see the other woman and her mother. From the mouth of this thin elderly woman, who is barely taller than the handle bars, comes a loud, demanding voice that surprises me. "I don't want that one. I want the one with vegetables."

In that moment, her daughter looks me in the eye, and I see not only her heavy heart, I see myself.

By the time we leave the store, my proud stoical mother is almost crying.

"Why are you crying?" I ask her.

"My foot hurts," she tells me.

I am dumbfounded. For all my intelligence and sensitivity, I didn't have a clue that her foot hurt. I thought her moans were an expression of her weakened muscles.

Exasperated I ask, "Why didn't you wear your comfortable sneakers?"

"They didn't match my outfit," she says.

There are times I am my mother's mother. Sometimes I am the loving mother who wants to gently rock her in my arms and soothe her like she did for me so many years ago. At other times, I am the critical mother, wanting her to get it together and function as she did when she was younger. I have come to see that in these moments of judgment, I not only cause myself distress, I pressure, embarrass, and shame her into thinking that she is less than the perfect being she truly is today. But most of the time, I am the daughter, learning from her, my first teacher. In all the colors and moods of her day, I learn the nuances of getting older. I see her retreat and fall down when life gets too much and I see her struggle back up and reemerge in all her beauty, humor, and kindness. At times when the lessons feel too big for me, I want to run away. But I choose instead to stay. In the quiet moments I find my humility, compassion, and humanity. I know that her soul is showing me these deeper aspects of myself. I am becoming whole in a way I didn't know was possible. This is my mother's gift to me.

Aimee Bernstein

No More Good-Byes

People living deeply have no fear of death.

Anais Nin

Saying good-bye was nothing new to my mom and me. We had been saying those words to each other for twenty-five years. As a young bride, I left home to start my married life on Long Island, New York. From there, my husband and I shifted to Arkansas, then Nigeria, back home to Tennessee, to Indiana, then Michigan, and finally as far away as Sydney, Australia, where we lived for twelve long years. Each happy visit home only led to another sad farewell. Each last embrace at the airport, another good-bye between mother and daughter.

In 1984, our family moved from Australia back to the United States to enroll our children in high school and finally settle down. We were in Texas only a year, however, when we received a call that Mama was on her way to the hospital, and in the words of her doctor, "Your mother's heart is slowly wearing out."

I cried, knowing it might not be long before we would be saying good-bye . . . again.

The sun streaming in Mama's hospital window was unbelievably golden, almost as if God was letting her enjoy a little of the Tennessee autumn without her ever having to leave her bed. Ward Five was quiet for a Saturday afternoon, and no one had come to visit all day. For two weeks there had been a steady stream of well-wishers at her bedside . . . preachers from all over Nashville, old church friends, neighbors and family, friends from her Garden Club, ladies from a birthday group, nieces, brothers, sisters . . . so many who had known her and loved her over the past sixty-eight years.

But today no one came, and so we sat there. Just the two of us. Mother and daughter. Alone.

"Mama, can I get you anything?" I asked.

"No, I'm fine. Just fine," she whispered.

I stood by her bed and took her hand in mine, rubbing her fingers while I asked again.

"Mama, please let me do something. Tell me something I can do for you."

She was quiet for a few seconds, gazing in the direction of the window. Then she turned her face toward mine and looked directly into my eyes.

"Wash my feet," she answered.

From under her bed, I pulled out a stainless steel wash pan. I poured a small amount of warm water into the pan and took a cloth and bar of soap from a drawer. Then I gently lifted the sheet and blanket, folded them back in an orderly fashion, and began to bathe the feet of my beautiful, aging mother.

"Mama?" I said. "You know what I'm thinking as I wash your feet?"

She shook her head from side to side, her eyes closed peacefully.

"Well, I'm just thinking about all the places these feet of yours have been. I'm remembering when you walked all us kids to church every Sunday, up the back alley instead of around the block to Sunday school. And I'm thinking of the day I followed you up the street to Mildred Reynolds's house to deliver a jam cake when she had a baby."

Without any warning, I realized I was right in the middle of saying good-bye again. But I gave in to the memories and let myself ramble on.

"I'm remembering a rainy day, Mama, when you drove me to school so I wouldn't get wet. We were running late, so you actually drove me there in your nightgown, no bra, and your house shoes barely touching the gas pedal."

She smiled . . . and I knew she was remembering right along with me.

"I remember the nursing homes where you walked room by room on Sunday afternoons, sharing flowers and communion with the elderly. I remember your trips to the hospital, back and forth, back and forth, during visiting hours. I remember the Meals on Wheels you cooked so that others could enjoy your meatloaf dinners. And I'm thinking of the day we popped in to see Mrs. Pippin . . . and you let me carry a coconut pie all by myself right up to her front door."

I paused to compose myself and wondered if she understood I was trying to give her the honor she so much deserved.

"And a few weeks ago," I continued, "as I was taking a casserole to one of my neighbors, I thought to myself as I was crossing the street, 'oh, my . . . I'm following in Mama's footsteps.'"

Then Mama and I couldn't say anything for a while because we both had tears in our eyes.

Mama died a few weeks later. My sister called to tell me she had walked into heaven on a Sunday afternoon. What calm filled my soul as I thought about my last good-bye. Oh, Happy Day! Mama now walks on streets of gold.

Charlotte Lanham

When God Takes the Mother . . .

Trouble is a part of life, and if you don't share it, you don't give the person who loves you a chance to love you enough.

Dinah Shore

I was in my early thirties, visiting my mother, when she leaned across the table conspiratorially, her eyes riveted on me, though seeming to be looking through me to her past. The urgency in her voice, a loud whisper, compelled me to listen rather than make a joke about her chest descending on the yolks of her two poached eggs. She told me she wanted me to know how she had survived World War II and why she did not go crazy. Although she acted like she was revealing a long-hidden secret, this would not be my first time hearing the story. Growing up, I had heard it often.

"If my mother did not tell me what she did," my mother continued, "I would not be here looking across the table at my grown daughter, now with a daughter of her own."

There was something different in the telling and the listening that morning just months after my daughter was born. I received the gift of my mother's story as I never had before, knowing that when she was old enough, I would share the story with my daughter. My mother's story is one of the most valuable gifts she has given me—in which she describes the most valuable gift her mother gave her, at a time when unfathomable despair—not invincible hope—might have been expected.

It was in the late 1930s in the village of Krazynstav that my grandmother, Simmah, called my mother into the small room that had been their "general store," a place for neighboring families to get flour, sugar, cloth, other staples, and occasionally special items like oranges brought by my grandfather from Lodz on one of his trips to buy cotton batting for the mattresses he sewed and sold. My grandfather was dead by then, their general store shut down by the Nazis. My grandmother closed the door separating this room from the rest of the small house and from my mother's young brothers and sister.

My mother did not want to hear the words she had been fearing and hoping would never come. She braced herself even before her mother told her she was to leave Krasynstav, that she could save herself and must; the next time the Nazis came through the village, they would leave no Jews behind. My mother, fourteen, had red hair, spoke Polish fluently, could pass, her mother told her. There would be no arguing, my mother knew looking at her mother's hands, trying to memorize the shape and length of the fingers, the texture of the skin, the way one of these hands she would never see again reached slowly into an apron pocket drawing out something. Her mother motioned her closer and lifted something over her head. It was a thin chain—with a cross hanging from it. Before my mother could utter her astonishment, she was silenced by her mother's finger upon her lips. My grandmother proceeded then to teach her how to cross herself, to kneel, and to say the Lord's Prayer in Polish, insisting she repeat it then—and from then on.

What happened next, my mother tells me, is what made it possible for her to survive the war; it gave her the will to live and the strength, again and again, to save herself when she wished instead to relinquish her life. Her mother pulled her closer and whispered into my mother's red hair, "Remember, when God takes the father and God takes the mother, God becomes the father and God becomes the mother. Talk to God, my child. You will never be alone. Talk to your God." These were the last words my mother heard from her mother's lips just before fleeing with the small valise her mother had already packed.

My mother did talk to God those first nights after fleeing, huddled in the forest or crawling to drink water from troughs on peasant farms. She talked to God while a maid in a prominent Polish family in which the eldest son, a seminary student who knew she was Jewish, hid her. She asked for God's protection constantly, mostly without moving her lips.

At night on her straw mat, she resisted sleep lest she call out to God in Yiddish and be overheard through the floor vents by the Nazis being entertained on the first floor. Later when she was moved to an abandoned barn and hidden beneath its floorboards, she continued to talk to God, begging not only to be kept alive, but also (because she believed her mother would wish it) that she be blessed with children one day.

My mother was blessed—with three children whom she has reminded continually to talk to God, telling them, "Even when you think you are alone, you are not. Even when you think no one is listening, you are never alone. Talk to your God."

My mother still talks to God and will until her last breath, I suspect. I talk to God all the time, too—even though my experience of God may not be the same as my mother's or that of my grandmother. My closeness to God as an inherent, abiding force of love has helped me to survive great darkness and trial as well, including almost losing my life after the birth of my daughter.

My mother is eighty-five as I write this. When she is no longer with us at all—when God takes the mother, I will cleave intimately to the gift of words and faith passed from my grandmother's lips to my mother's—the story I am giving my adult daughter—a gift with the power to illumine the dark from the inside out.

Ani Tuzman

She Never Left

To love is to receive a glimpse of heaven.

Karen Sunde

Mom had pancreatic cancer—a cancer with a low survival rate and one that typically kills within six months of its diagnosis. She had defied the odds, beating the disease for two and a half years, but that was just like my mom. She had an incredible attitude and a zest for living. Nothing could get her down. We were certain she would be among the 2 percent who survived, and we knew she was fighting hard for us.

She was admitted to the hospital in mid-November. We hoped she would be home by Thanksgiving, but one day without warning, she slipped quietly into a coma. A tumor had gradually worked its way around her spinal cord. She couldn't talk, but I was certain she could hear. I went every day to her bedside. Sitting beside her for hours, I gently stroked her hair—a gesture I knew she found particularly soothing. I sat stroking her hair and whispering softly over and over, "It's okay, Mom. It's okay if you need to leave. Everything will be all right."

I didn't mean it—not in my heart, not for a second. I said those words because I loved her and I didn't want her to suffer. I knew she worried about us all. I knew she held on for us. "It's okay, Mom. It's okay," I softly assured her. "Everything will be all right." Over and over I said those words to relieve her worries and make it easier for her to leave this world. Thank God, she could not see the tears that streamed down my cheeks as I spoke.

The first Friday of December, my husband and I worked late putting the finishing touches on a float for the upcoming Christmas parade. It was well past ten o'clock when we secured the last of the "snow" and hung the final stocking. We were exhausted as we left the warehouse and headed toward home, but I kept feeling a tug inside me, and despite the late hour, I told my husband, "We need to go by the hospital. I need to check on Mom."

As the elevator doors opened, my dad and sister were waiting. I knew immediately. My sister hugged me and said, "I wouldn't let them take her until you came." I don't know how my sister knew I was coming—maybe the same way I knew to come.

I went into the room alone and embraced my mom for the last time. I was thankful for that opportunity, but my heart ached that I had not been by her side earlier that evening. I couldn't believe that she had passed on and I had not been with her.

The flood of tears and sobs began while on our way home. My sorrow mixed with an overpowering fear. I shook uncontrollably, my teeth chattered incessantly. I was frightened, terrified realizing that the woman whom I had loved and depended upon since birth was now gone forever. The finality of it was too overwhelming. Wave after wave of intense shivers shook deep within me. I couldn't stop them.

At home I sought refuge in the shower, sitting down to

let the hot, steamy water pour down over my nerve-wracked body, but it provided no relief. I could not fathom life without Mom and the thought of it sent more tears pouring forth. All the while, my body continued to shake and shiver until I thought I would break apart.

My anguish continued until suddenly from seemingly nowhere, I heard a distinct whisper in my ear. "It's okay," I heard my mother say, her tone happy and upbeat. "Everything will be all right," she echoed my words to her.

I looked up to see her but saw no one, yet a sense of peace and calm embraced me. My body relaxed, the shivering and shaking ceased. It seemed she was gone as quickly as she had come, but the sense of love and peace lingered. I wasn't frightened anymore.

Her visit touched me deeply and meant so much. Those few words from her were all I needed to hear. I knew that she was all right and happy. I knew she had heard me, and I knew she was right—everything would be all right, for her and us.

Mom has been gone twenty years now and I still miss her dearly. Yet each time I recall her visit that night, my heart fills with an overwhelming love and peace, and I know that she is with me still. She never left.

Jean West Rudnicki

The Angel in My Arms

All God's angels come to us disguised.

James Russell Lowell

Seven weeks into my first pregnancy, I learned I was carrying twins. Like most expectant mothers, I proceeded through my pregnancy secure in the knowledge that I was doing everything "right." I ate well, had regular prenatal visits, took all my vitamins, and I didn't smoke or drink. Despite my best efforts, six months into my pregnancy, something went terribly wrong.

I sat in my doctor's office, pale-faced and quiet. This was my first pregnancy, but instinctively I knew something was not right. I was quickly escorted to a room ahead of his other patients, where he examined me and declared that I was in labor.

The attempts to stop my labor lasted forty-eight hours. After a long bedside vigil, my family had left upon my insistence that I was fine. An hour later, without warning, my water broke.

"Oh, no!" I screamed as I pressed the call button for my nurse. I was in sheer panic as I cried, "It's too soon!" The nurse asked how to reach my family. My mind became a jumbled whirl as I heard myself give my sister's number. Dana worked near the hospital, and within minutes she arrived, ready to be my coach.

"Breathe through the pain," Dana instructed. "Use short pants, like this—hee, hee, hee, hoooo, hee, hee, hoooo," she demonstrated.

"Oh, thank God you remember all this from Davey's birth," I said, feeling a little less scared.

"Davey's birth?" she retorted. "No way! I had a C-section. Actually, I got this from watching Bill Cosby."

Only my sister would take Lamaze lessons from a comedian. Forty-five minutes after my water broke, I delivered my first child—a daughter weighing in at one pound three ounces and just under twelve inches long. I named her Hayley. Dana promptly dubbed her the "little comet" because of her quick entrance into this world. I couldn't see Hayley through all the medical personnel swarming around her, but in the distance, I heard a faint cry that sounded more like the meow of a newborn kitten than that of a baby.

Dana ran to look and said, "She's beautiful!" Then, true to her comedic self she added, "She looks just like you—she's got huge feet!"

My laughter and joy over Hayley's birth was short-lived. A painful contraction jarred me back into the reality that I still had one more baby to deliver. I forgot to breathe and I began to shout, "Something's wrong!"

My doctor's report seemed cold and unemotional. Baby number two was in the breech position and the cord was prolapsing. He and my sister exchanged knowing glances, and he informed me that he would not do a cesarean in an effort to save the life of a baby that would probably die anyway. Suddenly, there was no more laughter. Nurses and doctors from the RICN continued their care and monitoring of Hayley while I waited in silence. Dana pulled a chair close to my bed, and never loosening her grasp on my hand, she whispered, "Do you understand what the doctor is saying?"

Silent tears rolled down my cheek as I shook my head from side to side.

"He means it's in God's hands now."

Moments later, I felt two hands inside of me, turning my baby around. I looked down and realized that no one was touching me. I slowly sat up and said nervously, "Something's happening." The intern assisting my doctor turned around just in time to deliver my second daughter—Hanna, whose name means "hope."

The excited intern announced that baby number two presented in the normal, head-first position. The cord was nowhere near her tiny neck.

"You were right," I cried to my sister. "She was in God's hands." From that moment on, I knew Hanna would survive.

Long, torturous days passed as I stared with envy when other moms in the unit bathed and fed their babies and gently rocked them to sleep, while I had to be content just holding my babies' delicate fingers and praying for them to grow strong. Nearly three weeks passed, lulling me into a false sense of security, and then Hayley contracted pneumonia. Helpless, I watched as she struggled to take each breath, her huge blue eyes staring back at me. I begged God not to take my baby from me, but she just kept staring at me with those eyes. Reluctantly, I whispered good-bye and told my precious firstborn it was all right to go. I swear she smiled at me, my little angel reassuring me in my time of utter despair.

Heart monitors and alarms were silenced as the doctor pronounced Hayley's death twenty-one days and nine hours after she burst into our lives. Her nurse, Marybeth, carried her still body into the family room where we were waiting and gently placed my daughter in my arms for the first time. She looked so peaceful wrapped in her white blanket. I'm holding an angel, I thought to myself. My perfect little angel.

People have often asked me, "Wasn't it hard holding Hayley after she died."

I always reply the same way, "Holding her was easy . . . letting her go was the hard part."

We buried Hayley on a brisk November morning. Our faith told us that God instantly welcomed her soul into his loving arms, so we celebrated the Mass of the Angels at her graveside. Later that evening, I returned to the RICN, where Hanna continued her struggle to survive. As I stared down at her I heard someone say, "Looks like Mom here could use a hug."

So many well-meaning people had hugged me so many times over the past three days that I turned like a robot waiting to accept the next offering of sympathy. I was surprised to see Marybeth standing next to an old worn oak rocking chair. "Have a seat," she ordered.

I sat in silence as she dressed Hanna in the smallest pair of pajamas I had ever seen. Carefully, she wrapped her in two heated blankets and securely taped the ventilation tubes that were helping my daughter breathe to the outside of the blankets. Gently, she lifted her from her shelter and placed her in my arms. "This is the best medicine for both of you," she added as tears streamed down her face.

As I cradled my baby in my arms for the first time, I was instantly met by two oceans of blue—Hanna's piercing eyes smiled at me just like her sister's, and I knew that Hayley was there looking out for her younger sister.

Nearly fifteen years have passed since the first time I held each of my babies. Hanna is a strong, healthy teenager now, thanks to the skill and love of so many people. Each day I thank God for bringing my daughters into my life, and every time I wrap my loving arms around Hanna, I remind myself how blessed I am to have held two beautiful angels in my arms.

Jodi Lynn Severson

6

LEGACIES AND MEMORIES

In every conceivable manner, the family is link to our past, bridge to our future.

Alex Haley

A Scrap of Paint

I sat in the driveway with a can of spray paint, ready to begin painting after sanding a few places that seemed rough. Then I stopped because my eyes were filled with tears. I wiped the tears away but they kept coming. Maybe I was allergic to the paint fumes? But I was outdoors with lots of fresh air. Something else was going on in my mind. It was that little chip of paint from the clothes hamper that was bringing back such powerful memories.

It was summertime in 1944, and my husband was in the Philippines as a Bomb Disposal Officer; I was staying with my mother and father in our rather primitive summer cottage in the Catskills with my six-month-old baby girl. Mother, as always, wanted things to be easy for me, and she knew that baby girls required lots of clean clothes and above all a place to put the dirty ones. I had never been noted for my neatness.

So first she found a nice box at the grocery store and covered it with contact paper and carefully put it in one corner of the bathroom for the clothes that I took off my baby. But soon with the door bashing into the box every time it was opened the box collapsed. We had specifications for what we needed: It must be small, no more than two feet high. It must have a lid that was easy to open and close, and it must be easy to carry around. Where would we find such an item?

While we looked we went through a series of boxes through the summer. As the war seemed to go on and on, we returned to Scarsdale and kept on looking. One day as I wheeled the stroller through the village, I saw the perfect hamper in a shop window. The size was perfect, it had a hinged top, and the color was a pale blue; and then I wondered about the price. I waited until Mother could be with me, and we went in and asked the price. It was certainly more than I could afford at that time, but Mother decided quickly that it would mean a lot to me over the hard months of loneliness and fear that lay ahead.

Now fifty-six years later, that same little clothes hamper sits in my bathroom and gathers the dirty clothes that my husband and I use. He returned unhurt from that long war, as so many others didn't. We had two more children and that hamper has been painted many times, used for our three children and eight grandchildren. The hamper outlived my mother, gone now for thirty-five years. For some reason, painting this old hamper one more time brought back the memories of that day we bought it. Mother has a way of entering into my thoughts with little messages of encouragement and love, and this time I knew she really appreciated the fact that she had bought a lovely, sturdy clothes hamper that has lasted for so many years. It is now white with a bargello cover in shades of blue, pink, and aqua. I wonder if my oldest daughter, for whom this old hamper first found a home, will claim it when I am no longer around. I hope she does, because every time she sees it, she may think of me as I think of my mother when I see it.

Julie Firman

The Gift of Having Something
to Believe In

*Far away in the sunshine are my highest inspi-
rations. I may not reach them, but I can look up
and see the beauty, believe in them and try to
follow where they lead.*

Louisa May Alcott

There is a lot to be said for believing in something. My
mother died when I was about two years old, but she has
never left me. I can honestly say I feel she has been with
me each and every day of my life.

There is a lot I don't remember from early childhood,
which is the case with many people. I do remember my
mother's soft face, her robe—quilted navy blue with a
bright red lining—and I remember her slippers sticking out
from the bottom of that full-length robe, I suppose because
I was still so very short at two years old. I remember the
smocked navy blue and green plaid dress I wore the day
my mother was laid out at our home—a great big casket
right there at the window side of our long dining room.

I even remember a time she was home but not well, and how my dad set her up on the patio outside. He carried her out and sat her on the chaise longue. I was amazed that my dad took the brass floor lamp out of the living room and set it up outside for my mom—right there next to where she was lying on the patio furniture, with the yellow and brown afghan. He plugged it in and turned it on after it got dark so she wouldn't have to go inside. I remember loving her being there outside—that happy and content feeling of playing where she could see me and some of my many brothers and sisters. (I was the youngest of seven surviving children.) Occasionally I would go running over and put my hands on her body underneath that golden yellow and brown blanket just to touch her and hold on to the moment. I learned later that this was one of her last visits home before she died in the hospital.

There is a lot that I don't remember from that time, which is probably why I cherish those recollections so very much. Mom died and we all kept growing up—my big brothers and sisters looked after me and took good care of me when our dad was at work. About five years later my father remarried (she also had seven children). Then I felt I had two moms—one in heaven, bowling with the angels during thunderstorms, and one here on earth. I called my stepmother Mom, and I still do.

One night my oldest sister was home with no Friday night plans. The rest of the huge family was out—except us two girls. I was about eight or nine and my sister was sixteen or seventeen. We were hanging out together in her bedroom just listening to the radio and talking, when she said, "I think you're old enough now."

"Old enough for what?" I asked.

She said, "Yes. You are old enough. You'll see. Just sit there."

She walked over to her jewelry box and dug around in it for a minute, which seemed like a long time since I was so curious.

"Here it is," she said.

"What?" I was so very curious, and I could not imagine what she was thinking I was old enough for that would be in her jewelry box. She looked somber, excited, and gentle all at the same time. She came and sat on the bed with me and asked me to listen while she kept feeling the object in her hands. I watched her and listened.

"Mom—our real mom—gave me something very special to give to you when I thought you were old enough to truly appreciate it. Can you believe it? It's true."

I was absolutely flabbergasted—amazed. My sister explained how our mom entrusted her with this special job and how she felt unsure when it would be the right time to present it to me. She needed to cry and so did I. But even as the tears were streaming down our cheeks, I couldn't stand the suspense any longer.

"Show it to me. Please."

When she released her hands, I opened mine to see a very small black velvet pouch. I carefully opened the neat spirally brass zipper while Judy was interjecting "Wait 'til you see!" Inside, I poured out the most beautiful solid silver rosary.

"It was blessed by the pope," she told me.

It was truly heavy with my mother's presence. I cried with joy and sadness all at once. I wasn't sure if I really was old enough to truly appreciate it that night. I did not feel deserving and I worried—what did my sister feel? My loving and gentle sister hugged me long and close and reassured me. Then we lightened up with amazement that our mother could be so thoughtful and clever. We felt her there with us. I said the rosary that night while lying in my bed before sleeping—and every night thereafter for years!

Now I am forty-two, the age my mother was when she died slowly of cancer. I feel sure my mother has been there with me every day of my life. Sometimes I reached out for her, talking to her as I went to bed. Sometimes she just showed up unexpectedly, like the time I was a volunteer at the hospital my mom died in, and I had the pleasure of meeting an extremely old nun who told me that she was with my mom when she was dying. My mother asked her, "Sister, will I be able to watch my children grow up?" To which the old nun replied, "Yes. Definitely."

And so she has.

Jennifer Gramigna

First Grandchild

An invite from the heart
"Please, be there, Mom,"
The main Event's
About to start.
This miracle of Life
Soon shows
Ten tiny fingers
Ten little toes.
Two lovely daughters,
Keri and Suzanne,
Working in tandem
Addressing God's plan
One the new mother
A nurse is the other,
Coaching, cajoling,
The clock slowly tolling.

I stand in the shadows
In awe of my "girls"
A Grandstand performance
More precious than pearls.
Each doing the job

The best way they know
And I in the wings
Applauding the show.
We witness it all
As the baby approaches
Encouraging, urging,
A room full of coaches.
Now comes the moment
The sweetness, the thrill
A new voice is heard from
That gives me a chill.
The Doctor, the Daddy,
Mom, Nurse, and Me
A sold-out production
We've all come to see.
A moment of wonder
With thoughts on my mind
How lucky am I
Having deep ties that bind.
An added attraction
Took place on that day
Not only a birth
But a new name to say—
"Grandma !"

Marilyn Bodwell

"I don't know, Mom . . . I'm just not a frilly white gown kind of bride. Maybe something in denim!"

My Mother's Face

Life began with waking up and loving my mother's face.

George Eliot

I've heard it all my life, "You look just like your mother." Not that I minded it. With red hair and "Wine with Everything" lipstick, Mama was as glamorous as a 1950s movie star. Though I've never been the glamorous type, there was no denying I had my mother's face—minus the lipstick.

Throughout her life, I observed an array of emotions on that face. When I was small, my mother's face often wore a wrinkled brow, reflecting her fast-paced determination to meet all the demands of caring for eight kids. As I grew older, her face revealed worry over problematic adolescents or my dad's unpredictable antics.

When I was a teenager, my mother's face mirrored her quick wit. Though I was never rebellious, I still thought myself pretty clever, and I certainly knew more than my mother did. At a very naïve sixteen, I came home from my job as a waitress and handed her a napkin on which a boy had written his phone number and invited me out on a date. "What do you think of this?" I asked, pleased that someone from school would find me attractive.

Her eyebrows arched as she tossed it back to me. "Use if for toilet paper," she quipped.

As a wife, I intentionally sought to wear my mother's face. She had me—her eighth child—on her thirty-fifth birthday. I had seven children by the time I was thirty-five. During those years, my mother's face beamed approval with each pregnancy announced. When everyone else was questioning my decision to have such a large family, I knew my mother would relish my news. After the arrival of each baby, my mother's glowing face was always one of the first I saw.

When my mother got cancer, I briefly lost sight of the beauty of her face. Distracted by mottled skin and the loss of her lovely red hair, I grieved at losing the mother I had always known. I mourned the inevitable altered course of life as this woman who managed her housework much like a Navy captain runs his ship now needed a walker to even saunter to the bathroom. As I trailed behind her to keep her steady, I reflected on how, without her hair, she had an uncanny resemblance to her own father. But during the months of caring for her, each time I drew eyebrows on her with pencil or assisted her with her lipstick, I began to see glimpses of my mother's face. And—whether through turban fashion shows or outrageous bathroom jokes—when her sense of humor again shone like a lighthouse during the greatest trial of her life, I saw her face as I had never seen it—so steadfast, so strong.

As the inoperable tumor in my mother's throat grew to the size of an orange, I watched desperation, panic, and anxiety—but never surrender—govern her face. "Go forward," she whispered with labored breath and raucous voice to the doctor's inquiry of the next step to take. She had much to live for, and to the end she wore her game face.

I was with her the night a simple breathing treatment triggered coughing, and her coughing evolved into choking. As I smashed the button to call the nurse, my mother's face was pure fear. As she mouthed, "I can't breathe, I can't breathe!" and the nurses rushed me out of the room, the look on her face is something I will never forget—it is stamped in my mind like a terrible song stuck on repeat. Though she lived thirty-six more hours, she remained unconscious.

I wasn't with my mother when she drew her last breath. Consequently, as I approached the doors of the funeral home, part of me feared seeing her lying lifeless in a casket. Then, as I crept toward her, I remembered her face. Deliberately ignoring her counterfeit hair that hid cancer's scars, shunning her hands so gnarled from fighting cancer's battle, I kept my eyes on her face.

The face that had guided me and given me strength. The face that personified determination both in life and in death. The face that I had always been told I had, but knew I could never have, really. As long as I live I will never quit trying to wear my mother's face.

Margie Sims

Hands of Time

*Because things are the way they are, things will
not stay the way they are.*

Bertolt Brecht

I saw it before I felt it. The metamorphosis. The evolu-
tion of my own hands into the hands of my mother. There
was no warning.

Graceful and elegant fingers that braided my hair, made
my lunches, and brushed away my tears belonged to my
mother so many years ago. Frightened animals stopped
quivering when she laid her hands upon them. Those
hands prepared our dinner, set the table, and then
scoured away the remnants left behind. They rolled pie
crust so delicate it would melt upon the tongue and
scrubbed stains from our clothes with a vengeance. The
iron pump handle yielded to her will, spilling cool water
into the bucket that hung from the spout.

Her nails were carefully tended by a monthly soaking in
warm soapy water followed by a firm scrubbing with a
small brush. An orange stick pushed the cuticles back, and
a file shaped their ovals to perfection. Occasionally a coat

of clear polish completed the ritual. Fancy scented creams were not an option—only the sensible healing ointments delivered by the Watkins man.

Throughout the years, I observed those beautiful hands as they ministered to the needs of our family. As time passed, her fingers picked up needle and thread, refusing to be idle. Under her touch, perfectly formed stitches matured into a plethora of colorful flowers, birds, and full-skirted ladies adorning pillowcases that cradled our heads at night. Her hand-stitched quilts grace the bedrooms of children, grandchildren, and great-grandchildren. Their beauty warms the soul as their weight warms the body.

Friends have told friends. From far and near the requests come for her hand-stitched wonders. Every stitch was done by hand whether creating a small pillow or a bountiful covering for a king-size bed. Each creation is unique, a one-of-a-kind treasure.

Arthritis has tried to stake a claim, but her fingers defy it, refusing to give way to defeat. The freckles on the backs of her hands slowly turned into "age" spots, screaming that it was time to slow down. The once smooth skin has become thinner, the veins playing peek-a-boo. But still her hands move, continuing to weave beauty with each new-born day.

My hands learned to braid hair, make lunches, and brush away tears. I held my hand out to feel the down of a bird, the sleek fur of a cat, the deep coat of a dog. With patience, I would hold out my hand until they would approach. Their quivering would stop when I placed my hands upon them.

My hands can set an elegant table for company and scour the burned pans from my culinary attempts. I learned to roll pie crust. I once scrubbed our laundry, before the modern convenience of an automatic washer became available. Though once I fought to draw water from the pump, today I turn a faucet and it appears, already warm or cold, depending on my choice. My hands pinned cloth diapers on babies and today peel off the tape to secure a disposable diaper on my grandchildren. My fingers grace the keyboard of a computer, weaving words, as my mother weaves her needle and thread.

Gathering my thoughts, I look upon my hands tonight and behold the spectacle. My mother's hands have transposed themselves to my own body. The fingers are still graceful, feeling from time to time the twinge of arthritis, but refusing to slow down. A plastic pump bottle of hand lotion sits at my fingertips to be used at my leisure. Still, the "age" spots have appeared, and I see the veins playing peek-a-boo. I'm not sure when it happened, but the metamorphosis is complete.

My only prayer is that the hands that belonged to me have left behind memories that will be recalled with pleasure when my daughters notice their hands have evolved into mine.

Carol Ann Erhardt

A Perfect Legacy

Perfectionism is the enemy of creation...

John Updike

I smiled with pride at the draft of my eighth grade research paper. The difficult work lay behind me. Only the task of typing remained. *How hard could it be to type a paper with footnotes?* I thought.

Over 100 footnotes to be exact. In my naïve zeal for good grades, I had created a research paper with a footnote for almost every sentence and unlimited possibilities for typing errors. If I accidentally omitted a footnote, I threw off the numbering sequence. If I underestimated how many sentences would fit on each page, I ran out of room at the bottom to cite all the footnotes. In either case, I saw no option in those precomputer days but to rip one mistake-filled page after another from my typewriter and retype them.

This paper has to be perfect. I fretted as my throat clogged with tears of frustration. *If it's not perfect, I won't get an A. If I don't get an A on this paper, I can't get an A in the class. Then I can't get straight As. I won't make the Highest Honor Roll or get a scholar certificate or see my name in the school paper or. . . .*

I didn't want to consider the consequences of imperfection. Good grades made me feel special. I craved the affirmation of words like "outstanding effort" written on an assignment. The possibility of receiving a lowly B sent me into panic.

"Having some problems with the paper?" my mom phrased the question delicately, while she noted the increasing volume of my moans and groans.

"Of course, I'm having problems!" I shouted at her as the tears finally broke loose. "Can't you see all these messed-up pages? Nothing's going right!"

I don't know whether Mom understood my answer through the ensuing jumble of words and tears, but she responded quickly once the sobbing subsided. "You're taking a break. I need to go to the store, and you're going with me."

Still trying to regain control of my emotions, I listened through a fog as my mom drove and talked. For some reason, she steered the conversation to families, reminding me of families known for their curly brown hair or long legs. She mentioned other friends who passed along their musical abilities or athletic skills from generation to generation.

Once we found a parking spot near the store, Mom cut off the engine and turned toward me with sudden seriousness. "You have a family legacy, too. It's called perfectionism, and it runs in my family. I come from a long line of people who tried to make everything in life perfect."

As shoppers passed by our windows, Mom and I sat in the front seat while she described family members like her Aunt Marjorie. Auntie didn't want anyone to help wash dishes at her house because she worried that they would be put away incorrectly. No matter how careful you were, Auntie would go behind you to turn all the cup handles in the proper direction and align the patterns on all the plates.

"My dad is just like his sister," Mom continued. "Everything has to be done a certain way. His way."

As young children, my sisters and I loved playing with the defective trophy parts in the back of Granddaddy's store. The box of rejects was always full because Granddaddy wouldn't sell a trophy that wasn't perfect. He expected excellence from everyone: himself, his employees, his wife, and his only child.

"I'm a perfectionist, too," Mom admitted. "You know that I can't leave home in the morning without making the bed. You see how I rush to vacuum the house before Peggy comes by, even though she's my best friend. I never allow you girls to use the dark blue towels because they have to look nice for company. I always want everything in the house to look . . . just right."

Mom grabbed my hand and held my eyes with her own. "And you're just like me. You've inherited my family's perfectionism, and that's why you've made yourself sick over this stupid paper."

Mom's voice choked as she searched for gentle words. "If you keep trying to do everything perfectly, you'll make yourself miserable, and you'll make everyone around you miserable. You'll drive everyone away. But you don't have to be like me or my family. You can reject your family legacy. It's your choice."

After a quick hug and a few more tears, Mom left me alone in the car to think while she went inside the store. Soon we returned home, and I went back to the typewriter.

I don't remember what grade I received on my research paper, but I have remembered my mother's words about our family's penchant for perfectionism. Her words come to mind every time I resent the growing pile of mail and papers on my kitchen counter or I open the door to a child's messy room. They play in my brain when I start to question my husband again about his half-finished repair project or obsess over choosing the right vacation spot.

I hear Mom's encouragement that I don't have to be like her. Some family legacies need to die. I can make that choice.

So I do. I grin and walk away thankful for messy rooms, unfinished projects, and the wonderful imperfection of my life.

Donna Savage

My Oldest and Dearest . . .

Every age can be enchanting, provided you live within it.

Brigitte Bardot

Mrs. Vick had been my mother's dearest friend. She'd been our neighbor for many years in the rundown apartment complex of the Portland suburbs. Neither woman had been in the best of health, both were dirt poor and barely able to pay their bills. They had formed a bond, of sorts, out of desperation.

When one was feeling well enough to make the half-mile walk to the store, there would be a knock on the other's door, asking if she needed food or maybe a prescription filled. When the end of the month neared and groceries grew short, cupboards would be opened, refrigerators emptied, and casseroles or pots of soup made with whatever ingredients were available between them. They laughed together over *I Love Lucy* and cried together over *All My Children*. In this way, two aging women, alone in the world except for the children they were raising on their own, found a way to survive.

When the power would go out in the dead of winter, we would bundle up in old quilts, troupe down to Mrs. Vick's apartment and huddle around her ancient kerosene heater. When summer baked the cracked sidewalks and weed-ridden dirt lawns, Mrs. Vick would bring a pitcher of iced lemonade and sit on the balcony of our second-story apartment with us, hoping to catch the errant breeze.

This was the way of things until my senior year in high school, when Mrs. Vick suddenly moved away. Her health had deteriorated until she was forced to move in with her eldest daughter. That fall, shortly before Thanksgiving, our seedy old apartment building caught fire and burned to the ground.

Everything we owned was consumed—clothing, furniture, and the few family heirlooms we possessed—when the ancient wiring finally gave out and ignited within the walls. The insurance company wrote us a small check, and Mother and I moved into a nearby rental house. Shortly afterward, following a long battle with her failing kidneys, Mother passed away. I grieved, of course, but I knew that she was happy to be free from her twice-weekly dialysis regimes, which had come to be a nightmare for both of us.

Three years later I was finishing nursing school and had taken a night position at a local elder care facility. As I made the morning rounds with my medication tray, the name on the door of room 201 caught my eye: Elizabeth Vick. I knocked softly on the door and entered. Sure enough, it was the same Mrs. Vick who had shared our struggles through all of those summers and winters. Her white hair was thinning, and her frail hands shook with palsy now, but the same tough, resilient spark shone in her eyes. She remembered me, of course, and was over-joyed to have me sit at her bedside and talk about the "old days" with her. I spent many breaks and lunches in room 201, reading Mrs. Vick the latest letter from her daughters and telling her about the comings and goings of my life, to which she listened with rapt attention.

One day I mentioned the fire that had destroyed all of our belongings, and Mrs. Vick suddenly began to cry, small tears slowly tracking down her weathered cheeks. She pointed to the small closet on the far wall of her room and told me to look inside the cardboard box in the far corner. Inside were a number of old keepsakes, including a cheap cardboard photo album. This she asked me to bring to her, which I did, and she turned the pages slowly until she found the one she was looking for, then handed the album to me.

Now it was my turn to cry! There, under a yellowing sheet of plastic, were the only four remaining pictures of my mother to exist anywhere. Two were summer shots of the balcony (both taken by me with Mrs. Vick's old Konica), the third was of my twelfth birthday party, and the last picture was from an early Christmas. In this last photo, I sat in my mother's lap, smiling hugely; her arms were wrapped tight around my tiny shoulders, and her head rested against my own. On her face was the sweet smile that sometimes seemed so hard to remember.

With a trembling hand, Mrs. Vick removed the old photo from the book and handed it to me. "Sometimes," she whispered, "God makes us find our gifts from him. I never would have remembered these pictures if you hadn't come and sat with me every day."

I leaned down and took her frail body in my arms, our tears mingling as I squeezed her as hard as I dared. That was almost three years ago. I've switched jobs twice, and moved once, but I've never forgotten Mrs. Vick. I still drive out to that nursing home two or three times a week.

In the summer, when the air conditioners in the new building make the rooms just a little too cool for her failing circulation, I'll bring bottles of sugar-free lemonade, and we'll sit on the shady veranda and watch the Columbia River roll by. We read letters from her daughters (and granddaughters), talk about life as it used to be, and sometimes we just sit and enjoy the warmth.

On my desk at home sit three frames. The largest, in the center, holds my nursing certificate. To the right is a small photo of a smiling little girl in her mother's lap, and on the right is that same child, many years later, sharing a lemonade with her oldest and dearest friend.

Betty Perkins as told to Perry P. Perkins

Gifts of Love

*Of all nature's gifts to the human race, what is
sweeter than children?*

Marcus Tullius Cicero

On my way to check out at the bookstore, a rack of
stuffed animals caught my eye. I stopped to admire the
display of bunnies with long floppy ears and casual poses.
Their cheerful faces conjured up bittersweet memories of
our home littered with stuffed animals when our two
daughters were small. Long before they reached their
twenties they had given away most of the furry toys,
keeping only the special ones tucked away. Our youngest,
now in college, still had a few favorites on display in her
room, though.

"I'll get her a bunny," I said to myself as I held one close.
I put it back. "What does a twenty-year-old need with a
stuffed animal?"

I fingered the multicolored ribbon around its neck. Our
daughter's junior year of college had been very stressful,
full of work and performing and demands on her time and
energy—and niggling worries about what she would do

with her life postcollege. Sometimes I worried, too. Have I done all I can to support her? I bought the rabbit.

A few days later she called. "I'm coming home for the night. I need to see you and Dad, the dogs, to sleep in my own bed."

That evening when she settled in her room to study for a test, I gave her the bunny.

"Something you can cuddle at school—and it's dust free," I joked. (She's terribly allergic to dust.)

She laughed, holding the bunny close. "You guys." Her smile hinted at memories of other treasured surprises given to her out of love. She set it on her lap, between her and her books. It stayed there while she studied and slept with her that night. And it made the journey back to college with her the next day.

A few days later I was hunting for a T-shirt in my dresser. Tucked away in one corner, a little stuffed teddy bear looked up at me. I pulled out the white bear and stroked her satin angel wings. A smile crossed my face as I straightened her necklace and read again "Mom" written on its red felt heart.

Three years ago my mother was very ill. I shuttled back and forth between California and Illinois to spend as much time with her as possible. My emotions shuttled back and forth, too: between my responsibilities to my own family and the need to spend time with her during her last days. My husband was commuting from California to Massachusetts every two weeks or so, and our youngest daughter was still in high school. There just wasn't enough time, or enough of me, for all of this.

One of my brothers lived close to Mom so we took turns being with her. I struggled with my feelings near the end of my week with her. I wanted to stay, to be there for this dear woman who had been there for me for over fifty years. I wanted to be with my daughter and my

husband—my family now—who needed me as much as I
needed them.

Mom would be the last one to question my going. "You
can't have your cake and eat it, too," she always used to
tell me when I was growing up.

I wandered through the hospital gift shop on my way
back from lunch. "What can I leave her as a token of my
love?" She already had a shelf full of family photos and a
houseful of treasures and knickknacks. I knew what she
wanted most was my company and I'd given her that. I
wished I could give her more.

A rack of stuffed angel-bears caught my eye. Hesitantly
I picked up the one with "Mom" written on its red heart.
What will an eighty-one-year-old woman do with a stuffed bear? I
put it back. Still, it felt like the right thing to do. I bought it.

"A little angel to watch over you and to help you
remember how much I love you." I gave her the bear.

She smiled and cuddled the bear in her hands. I gave
her a bear hug myself and left for my flight back to
California.

A week or so later my brother called. "I think it's time,
Susan. You better come soon."

He picked me up at the airport and brought me up-to-
date on Mom's health since we last talked. At the hospital
I hugged her tight.

"I thought I heard you several times, coming down the
hall," she said. "Your voice, your walk."

"I'm here now." I squeezed her cool hand, the skin as
smooth and translucent as fine porcelain.

She picked up the angel-bear from the bedside table. "I
slept with him last night."

My mom died a few days later.

I traced the edge of the bear's red heart and slipped it
back into its cozy corner in my T-shirt drawer. I thought
about my mother, my daughters, and all those precious

memories grown from bears and bunnies, from unexpected and treasured words and gestures. Whether it's something I hold in my hand or something I hold in my heart, gifts of love circle from daughter to mother and mother to daughter through the generations.

Last night my daughter called to update me on her résumé. We talked about her day and mine, about the songs she is preparing for her big concert next month.

"I'm so looking forward to being home this long weekend," she said.

"We'll see you Thursday evening."

"By the way, Mom, thanks again for the bunny. I slept with him last night."

Susan Rothrock Deo

Fifty Dollars

*A person's wishes and prayers are only grati-
fied and answered when they harmonize with
one's thoughts and actions.*

James Allen

New York City can make you paranoid. So when I saw the
elderly couple staring at us and talking, I was sure WE were
the subject of their conversation. But being a sensible
woman, I ignored them and continued to shop at the grocery
store with my mother, who hadn't even noticed the couple.

And she looked rather puzzled when the woman spoke
to her, saying: "You don't remember me, do you? I owe
you fifty dollars."

A blank look crossed my mother's face.

Then the husband spoke up. "You're the guardian angel
who got my wife through the days when I was in the hospital. Not only did you feed her body but also you fed her
soul."

And then my mother remembered. As she later told me,
she had been at this same grocery store when she noticed
a woman walking slowly along the aisles and crying. Most

of us would have gone on our way, but my mother is never afraid to reach out a helping hand. She doesn't think about possible rejection or even risk but approaches strangers in need openly and lovingly and lets them react as they will.

She had gone up to this woman and said, "You look so sad. Can I help?"

The woman, more appreciative of a fellow human's kindness than of any possible help for her problem, poured out her story. Her husband had become ill suddenly and might not even live. She had no money available because he handled all their finances and there had been no time to plan. She was worried about him and also about herself and was trying to figure out what she could afford to eat.

My mother had listened and offered comfort, then held out a fifty-dollar bill. The woman protested at first, but my mother was able to convince her that people help one another in need and that repayment comes through others as kindness circulates throughout the world.

The woman accepted the money, bought herself food, and that was the end of it. My mother had never seen her again—until today.

The husband again mentioned that the act of generosity had not only enabled his wife to eat but also had bolstered her faith in life and humankind. And he said he hoped to repay the money someday.

My mother said, "The money isn't important. Caring for each other is."

The couple accepted that graciously and went on their way, smiling and holding hands. I smiled a lot, too, because this was MY mother. It's easy to write a check to charity but much harder to reach out to a stranger in public. The woman was blessed by her chance encounter with my mother as I am blessed to be my mother's daughter.

Frances Salorio

$\overline{7}$

THANK YOU

Daughters do wonderful things.
Not the wonderful things you expected them
to do.
Different things.
Astonishing things.
Better than you ever dreamed.

Marion C. Garretty

"Your hugs are the nicest
hand-me-downs, Mom."

A Mother's Sacrifice

An ounce of mother is worth a pound of clergy.

Spanish Proverb

One hundred dollars . . . every year my grandpa would give my mom $100 the first week of December for her to buy whatever she desired. This had been a tradition ever since I could remember.

Although everywhere I looked was decorated in anticipation of Christmas, my sister and I were dreading Christmas this year. We knew that Dad's business had been doing terribly and that there would be little money for gifts. My mother had been a stay-at-home mom so that she could spend ample time with her children . . . so Dad's income was all that we had to rely on.

It was quite depressing getting the stores' advertisements in the mail. Everything seemed so enticing, and I was allured by the beautiful new fashion styles that were out. Of course, it was vital to a teenager to get new clothes for Christmas. We would strut in our new clothes around the high school like vain runway models in hopes that no one else had received the same new outfits that we had.

I wanted Christmas to be over so badly. I wished that it wouldn't come at all. Mom took us shopping one day after school. I didn't know what her purpose was unless to drive us even farther into the depths of despair. She took me to my favorite clothing store. I found a dress that was beautiful. It was very classy, and I was sure I would look very distinguished if I had it. I tried it on. It was amazing . . . like no other dress I had ever owned before. It was as though it was hand designed for me. I stared in the dressing room mirror, absorbed in thought. I came back to reality when a knock on the door interrupted my thoughts. "Jennifer, how does it fit? Let me see it on you," my mom said.

I walked out of the dressing room in complete confidence that I was the belle of the ball. "Mom, I love it. It is perfect. Don't you agree?"

"Yes, it's beautiful. Purple is your color. Would you like to try anything else on?"

"No," I said. "That's it!"

We left the store that day empty-handed. I knew Mom didn't have the money for it, but I couldn't get that dress out of my mind. This was the first year we didn't go out and buy a Christmas tree. I knew that money was really tight. My brother got a Charlie Brown Christmas tree out of the front yard and brought the twig that we called a tree into the house. It didn't take long to decorate the twig. This was going to be the worst Christmas ever.

One day when Mom came out of her bedroom, I noticed the condition of her shoes. They had holes in them. I hadn't ever noticed them before. She had been wearing them in the cold winter without any complaints. Her panty hose had holes in them. Apparently it had been a long time since she had bought new ones. Soon, my dress became less and less important. My mother was going without, and yet her concerns were for us. I never heard her wish list or what she wanted for Christmas. I guess I was so absorbed with myself that I didn't take time to ask.

It was Christmas day. There were no presents under the tree. We gathered around the table and gave thanks to God for our breakfast. Dad began to tell funny stories, and soon we began to give reasons why we were thankful. In a short period of time, I began to forget how "awful" Christmas was. Mom disappeared and came out her bedroom door bursting with excitement.

"Well, time for presents!" she exclaimed.

She handed each of us one present. I opened up mine. It was the dress. I began to cry uncontrollably. I knew that Mom had spent her Christmas money—her $100 from her dad—to buy us each a gift. We each opened our one gift that day. Soon we were all crying and hugging.

The dress has been worn over and over again and is now no longer in my possession. Perhaps I gave it to Goodwill or sold it in a yard sale, but the sacrifice that my mom made and the positive attitude that she displayed has lived on in my heart.

A mother doesn't have to put her children's needs above her own. A mother doesn't have to make sacrifices or seek to bond with her children, but mine did. That is what has made her more than my mother; she has become my friend.

Jennifer L. Smith

Always a Mom

Character is the architecture of the being.

Louise Nevelson

Too bad my artist's eye is hampered by chimpanzee hands. I'll never be able to re-create my favorite memory of Mom at her best. It was late afternoon and she'd just stepped out of the car after a full day's work. Dressed in a straight skirt and heels, she approached my friends and me and, without a word, merrily jumped the length of our hopscotch grid. If only I could catch her mischievous grin and record it on canvas. If only I could give her bright blue eyes that same sparkle and her wavy brown hair that same in-flight appearance. Imagine how many other forty-year-old mothers might find inspiration and wonder if they could exhibit the same joy and enthusiasm after eight hours at the office.

That moment captured my mother's heart and the essence of motherhood. No matter what else she was—wife, daughter, sister, friend, seamstress, or top-level secretary—Mom was always a mother. She must have had times when she was too tired, too busy, or too irritable to nurture one of her kids, but I don't remember ever being turned away. I knew she always welcomed my company. She enjoyed being a mother.

Like the rest of us women, she had no idea how to raise children. Even today, when advice abounds, no one really knows how to raise children because every child is an individual. How can you write a formula for each individual? My older sister was compliant and easygoing, but my two brothers were headstrong and rebellious. My feelings were eggshell fragile, and life with me was a series of omelets. Where's the formula for raising a mixed brood like ours?

Love, of course, is the first order for every parent, but how do moms express love to each child as he or she needs it? The stern words necessary to corral my brothers would have sent my sister into isolation and left me sobbing for hours. So how did Mom do it? How did she manage to raise four kids and still have enough energy to jump through numbered squares at the end of a long day? Maybe being a mom, and loving it, energized her.

I wonder if she worried and felt the heavy weight of responsibility to transform four self-centered youngsters into upstanding citizens. Did she ever wish for a few hours alone or dream of the day when she and her husband would be John and Edith instead of Dad and Mom?

I know she didn't give up her dream of a perfect figure. I remember her kneading her thighs with a rolling pin every summer in vain effort to discourage flab.

And she never lost her love of creativity. She delighted in crafts of all kinds and took up cake decorating in her fifties. Painting classes in her sixties resulted in the beautiful watercolors that grace almost every room of my home. My chimpanzee hands weren't inherited from her.

Today Mom is eighty-seven. Crafts, baking, and fine arts no longer fill her days, but her nurturing heart beats as strong as ever. An hour with her great-grandkids makes her happier than anything else. Even though shopping is not her favorite activity, she loves to send me out in search of perfect gifts for Nick, Emma, Joe, and baby Lizzie. While two-year-old Joe is too wiggly for her to hold, she's happy to use every ounce of strength in her hands to cuddle Lizzie. She's still a mother at heart.

Now that I've known the joys and trials of motherhood and the delight of being a grandmother, I appreciate my mother more than ever. Her even temper, her sense of humor, and even her nagging were different ways to say "I love you." So was hopscotch.

June Williams

Love Conquers All

Plant love, harvest happiness.

T. J. Mills

Trudging the two short blocks home from work that cold and blustery January afternoon, my mind was busy planning for the birth of my first child, just three weeks away. I still needed so many baby things, and fitting them into the budget on a private's salary wasn't easy.

In fact, this whole parent thing was a bit daunting. I felt ill prepared, but Mom reassured me, "Love is strong, stronger than anything. It conquers all. Your love for your baby will outweigh your fears." Smiling, she reached out and gently touched my face, tucking a stray lock of hair behind my ear.

"Honey," my mother continued, "where is your faith that everything happens for the best? God's in charge and he knows what he's doing. He loves us and knows what's best for us. He created this child you are carrying and chose you to be its mom."

Turning the corner, my reverie was interrupted. I stopped short, startled to see our car in the driveway. Ted wasn't due home for several hours. Puzzled, I hurried up the steps, pulled open the door, and called out, "Whatcha doing home so early?" Midway in the process of shedding my coat, I looked up to see both Ted and my parish priest, their expressions somber.

"Sit down, honey." Ted nudged me toward the sofa and knelt beside me.

My eyes wide with fear, I croaked, "What is it? What's happened?"

Ted hesitated, then tearfully and gently whispered, "Mom died this morning."

"No! Not Ma." Visions of the portly grandmother who had been a second mother to me filled my mind. Knowing that, at age seventy-eight, she had lived a long good life did nothing to ease the pain.

"No, honey. Pat, your mom, died this morning. Not your grandmother."

"What?" I lifted my head from my hands, comprehension eluding me.

"It's Pat, honey."

"No, she's too young. She's not even a grandmother yet." I patted my bulging tummy as if the fact that I had not yet given birth proved my mother still lived, but Ted's cheerless eyes told me differently.

Tears dissolved into sobs as the realization sank in that my child would never know his grandmother. We had so many plans, Mom and I. She was coming to help me when the baby was born.

Fr. Bob's voice came to me from a great distance. "I didn't know your mom, but knowing you, I know she was a great mom and would have been a wonderful grandmother, too. She wouldn't want you to do anything to harm the baby, least of all to let your grief over her cause you so much upset that this little one comes too early."

I knew his words to be truth and fought to control my

emotions. We talked about how relationships don't end with death, but are only changed, about how my child would have someone special in heaven praying for him, and about how much my mom loved this child already. Mom's words about love conquering all came back to me. How could love overcome death?

The funeral passed in a blur. The decisions that come with an unexpected death were somehow made. This longest week of my life was surreal. But the new life I was nurturing stayed safely tucked in my womb in spite of the mourning, the stress, the lack of sleep.

It was a comfort to know that my mother was so well thought of. The church was overflowing with people and flowers. The condolences were sincere and heartfelt. But I was relieved to return to our tiny duplex, hoping the ordinary would allow me to think of something else. But it was not to be. Each time my child moved within my womb, I was reminded that my mother wouldn't be there for the birth. "I need you, Mom," I whispered. How could I shop for the rest of the baby things without her? How could I raise a child without her?

Ted worried that my grief was intensifying, instead of abating. Ted worried about our child, and he, too, grieved for my mom, who had adopted him as her own. He didn't want to go to work that first day back, but I insisted. Yet, when the door closed behind him a loneliness unlike any I had ever known settled on me, a physical ache that caused me to hunch over. I missed my mom.

When the doorbell rang, I didn't want to answer it. I knew my eyes were red and puffy, and I sure didn't feel like talking to anyone. A second ring, followed by a loud knock brought me to my feet. "Postman," called out an unfamiliar male voice. "I've got a package for you." In my depressed mood, the wide smile on this stranger's face was an affront. Neither my appearance nor my glumness deterred him.

"This box is way too big to leave on the porch," he offered. "Somebody must love you. Maybe it's a late Christmas present." He obviously enjoyed playing Santa.

Taking the box, I managed a smile and thanked him. Kicking the door shut with my foot, I glanced for the first time at the return address and immediately recognized Mom's handwriting. My mouth fell open, and I gulped in a sharp ragged breath. I sank to the floor, back to the door, and with trembling fingers, unwrapped the package.

Baby stuff! All I would need—gowns, diapers, receiving blankets, sweaters, booties, stuffed animals, rattles, and more. I was crying again, but these were different tears. They were the tears that come with the assurance that you are loved. The dam that broke within me flooded my soul, washing me clean. My bittersweet tears confirmed Mom's words, "Love conquers all." I could just hear her saying, "These are for my grandchild, whom I love with all my heart. This child of my child is precious to me, as you are. Know that I love you both for all eternity."

Nancy Baker

"She ate it. I guess love DOES conquer all."

How Sweet the Sound

You don't choose your family. They are God's gift to you, as you are to them.

Desmond Tutu

The lead should have been mine. All my friends agreed with me. At least, it shouldn't have been Helen's, that strange new girl. She never had a word to say, always looking down at her feet as if her life were too heavy to bear. What's up with that anyway? We've never done anything to her. We think she's just stuck up. Things can't be all that bad for her, not with all the great clothes she wears. She hasn't worn the same thing more than twice in the two months she's been at our school.

But the worst of it was when she showed up at our try-outs and sang for my part. Everyone knew the lead role was meant for me. After all, I had parts in all our high school musicals, and this was our senior year.

My friends were waiting for me, so I didn't hang around for Helen's audition. The shock came two days later when we hurried to check the drama department's bulletin board for the play postings.

We scanned the sheets, looking for my name. When we found it, I burst into tears. Helen was slated to play the lead! I was to be her mother and her understudy. Understudy? Nobody could believe it.

Rehearsals seemed to go on forever. Helen didn't seem to notice that we were going out of our way to ignore her. I'll admit it; Helen did have a beautiful voice. She was different onstage somehow. Not so much happy as settled and content.

Opening night had all its jitters. Everyone was quietly bustling around backstage, waiting for the curtain to go up. Everyone but Helen, of course. She seemed contained in her own calm world.

The performance was a hit. Our timing was perfect, our voices blended and soared. Helen and I flowed back and forth, weaving the story between us. I, the ailing mother praying for her wayward daughter, and Helen playing the daughter who realizes as her mother dies that there is more to this life than this life.

The final scene reached its dramatic end. I was lying in the darkened bedroom. The prop bed I was on was uncomfortable making it hard to stay still. I was impatient, anxious for Helen's big finish to be over.

She was spotlighted upstage, the grieving daughter beginning to understand the true meaning of the hymn she had been singing as her mother passed away.

"Amazing grace, how sweet the sound. . . ." Her voice lifted over the pain of her mother's death and the joy of God's promises.

"[T]hat saved a wretch like me. . . ." Something real was happening to me as Helen sang. My impatience left.

"I once was lost but now I am found. . . ." My heart was touched to tears.

"[W]as blind but now I see." My spirit began to turn

within me, and I turned to God. In that moment, I knew his love, his wishes for me.

Helen's voice lingered in the prayer of the last note. The curtain dropped. Complete silence. Not a sound. Helen stood behind the closed curtain, head bowed, gently weeping. Suddenly, applause and cheers erupted, and when the curtain parted, Helen saw her standing ovation.

We all made our final bows. My hugs were genuine. My heart had been opened to the Great Love. Then it was over. The costumes were hung up, makeup tissued off, the lights dimmed. Everyone went off in their usual groupings, congratulating one another. Everyone but Helen. And everyone but me.

"Helen, your song, it was so real for me." I hesitated, my feelings intense. "You sang me into the heart of God."

Helen gasped. Her eyes met mine.

"That's what my mother said to me the night she died." A tear slipped down her cheek. My heart leapt to hers. "My mother was in such pain. Singing 'Amazing Grace' always comforted her. She said I should always remember that God has promised good to me and that his grace would lead her home."

Her face lit from the inside out, her mother's love shining through. "Just before she died she whispered, 'Sing me into the heart of God, Helen.' That night and tonight, I sang for my mother."

Cynthia Hamond

Bonus Mom

*Challenges are what make life interesting;
overcoming them is what makes life meaningful.*

Joshua J. Marine

"You don't love my family as much as you love yours,
and you don't treat us all the same."

This emotional outburst from my sixteen-year-old stepdaughter stopped me in my tracks. *Where had these hurtful
words come from? What had I done to cause her to be so upset with
me that she would lash out in such anger?*

I was crushed, deeply hurt, and in complete disbelief
that she would even confront me this way. No doubt she
resents me for marrying her father only a year after her
mother passed away. And now she's part of a blended
family of seven children. I realize it's a big adjustment for
her, for all of us. What is in her heart? How can I reach her?

Days following her outburst, she was still withdrawn and
not very communicative, but it was obvious her attitude
was a little better. *What made her change? Had the outburst
helped release her frustration with this new family arrangement—
and with me?* Whatever it was, I was thankful for it.

I tried to get close to her, to at least be her friend. It was okay that she didn't call me Mom as her younger brother and sister did. I knew I wasn't really the "wicked stepmother" that I felt like when I was around her, but I still wondered if she saw me that way.

By the time she went away to college our relationship showed signs of improvement. She married and began a family, and somewhere during that time, became a Christian. Both her life and attitude began to improve. Then one day, she took me by surprise.

"I'm sorry for the way I treated you when I lived at home. Will you please forgive me?"

Tears filled my eyes as she spoke.

"Yes, of course I will," I said.

I asked her to forgive me for anything I might have done to hurt her. She couldn't respond, but with tears in her eyes, gently nodded her head yes. We hugged for a long time. I'm so glad for the change in her. What a neat young woman she has become.

This was the beginning of a relationship that would only improve with time. Yet I sensed she still struggled with who I was to her. Obviously I was not her birth mother, although I had always done "motherly" things with and for her. She could introduce my husband and me as her parents, but I knew it was still difficult for her to introduce me as her mom. It didn't matter to me how she referred to me. Our relationship had improved so much that now we were friends, and to me, that was the most important thing of all.

But just recently I was sitting with her in church. The pastor asked everyone to turn to their neighbor and share something for which they were thankful.

She turned to me, patted my arm, and said,

"I'm thankful for—my bonus mom."

Joanne Schulte

The Grandmother of the Bride: When Gratitude Trumps Guilt!

At times our own light goes out and is rekindled by a spark from another person. Each of us has cause to think with deep gratitude of those who have lighted the flame within us.

Albert Schweitzer

The first time there was a wedding in our family, I was careful not to tax my aging mother with the details. "Everything's working out fine," was my standard response to her questions about the plans, even on days when I felt inches away from a nervous breakdown. Home weddings can do that, even to the most stalwart mothers of the bride, but I certainly didn't want to worry mom . . . and I'm lousy at asking for help.

On the day of our oldest daughter's wedding, my mother—her grandmother—appeared in the beautiful, sky blue dress, walked proudly down the aisle, and had one of the finest days of her life.

Only later did I sense a certain vague regret on her part

that it had all gone so quickly, and that she had somehow missed the texture of the experience.

I thought about that a lot when our next daughter announced her engagement two years later. I thought about how precious these years are with Mom, and how long and empty her days must sometimes be in her small apartment in a city high-rise.

I thought about the look on her face on that first granddaughter's wedding day, a look that somehow blended pride, pleasure, excitement, and incredible joy.

And, yes, I thought about how much I could use the help in staging one of life's monumental events.

First, I discussed a startling notion with the new bride-to-be herself, a pressured graduate student with an impossible schedule: How about if Mom-mom, who had both time on her hands and a great natural ability to get information from the most reluctant, got involved in some of the preliminary planning? How about if she, for example, did the research about the availability of spaces for the wedding?

Nancy was startled. Mom-mom as initial wedding coordinator? Could she handle it? Would she want to? And how would I, presumably the chief of operations, feel about relinquishing the title?

As I told Nancy, I realized that I wouldn't mind a bit! As a full-time freelance writer, I'm constantly grasping for time, and frankly, the prospect of days and days on the phone with hotels and country clubs, public buildings and historic sites did not exactly gladden my heart.

So it was with some trepidation, but also great curiosity, that we began our noble experiment. Mom-mom was unleashed on the world of weddings, and we waited breathlessly to see what would happen.

Within a week, my mother had done more than any human being could be expected to do. She had made careful lists, with the help of the local library, of all possible public buildings that permit weddings. She had assembled a similar list of acceptable hotels and clubs. She had phoned each and every prospect and elicited information that many are not prone to give over the phone, playing up her "I'm a sweet little old lady" persona. She had even, bless her, headed out on foot to scope out the places she could and had made scores of calls to her lady friends to get "references" on this or that facility.

It was at once impressive, touching, sweet, amusing—and unbelievably helpful. My octogenarian mother was clearly soaring on the challenge and looked and sounded younger than she had in years.

Through the whims and winds of change, my mother was a vital and integral part of the wedding planning. When we ditched the idea of weddings at hotels or public spaces and opted again for the pleasures—and perils—of a home wedding, she was there to cheer us on and say, "It will be perfect!"

When the question of which caterer would be hired to coordinate the day, from first hors d'oeuvre to last slice of wedding cake, Mom stood by listening to the pros and cons, offering her wisdom, and reminding us that nobody would remember precisely how the carrots were done by the next morning. Maybe it takes eighty-four years on this earth to gain that perspective, but we needed it and welcomed it.

Still, if Nancy was wistful about place cards with violets around the border, her grandmother found them. If I was ready to surrender and choose a dress for myself that is not exactly what I'd hoped for, my mother was there to remind me that this is a very special day, and that good things come to those who . . . search!

In our garden on a June day at high noon, Nancy wed her wonderful Michael.

They recited their vows near the gate from which

Nancy and her sisters had swung, in violation of all household rules. They danced their first dance and toasted each other standing on ground that had known the bride's feet not in satin slippers with rosettes, but in sturdy little sneakers.

And, oh, how right it all seemed.

Not only was the bride radiant that day, but also her grandmother. There was a new sparkle in my mother's wise green eyes and a new bounce in her step.

Nancy's wedding had linked our three generations in an extraordinary way. It had taught me that there's no shame in asking for and accepting help from the one person in the world who will always give it unstintingly, wrapped in love.

Yes, Mom-mom power is awesome.

Just ask a daughter who finally learned to accept help with gratitude instead of guilt.

Sally Friedman

The Gift

Ker-splat!

"Mama . . . I dropped another bottle." The broken glass lay on the floor along with the puddled milk.

"It's okay, Flossie," Mama called out from the bedroom. "Just go to the ice box and get a fresh one. Eloise ain't had enough t' eat."

I guess a seven-year-old feeding her baby sister on an icy, winter night might sound unusual, but not in 1920. People did what they had to do to survive. I slid off the chair, pushed the mess aside, and clunked around in Mama's shoes, intent on performing my big girl duties. I placed the new bottle in a pan of water on the stove, then took Daddy's poker and stoked the coals extra hard, just the way he'd taught me. Flames shot up, burning in a golden red halo. I shivered and moved in closer.

When the bottle felt warm enough, I set the pan aside. Eloise lay in bed sucking on a bluish, big toe. "C'mon, sis. You're not finished yet."

With only one bottle left, I dared not go to sleep again. I squinted out the window, my eyes searching the soupy, gray cloak of dawn. A passing train's monster wheels glinted in the light and its engine belched. Clack-clack-whoosh, clack-clack-whoosh. Neighbor men ran up, climbed aboard, and jumped from car to car, throwing off all the coal they could manage. Then they hopped down, picked up their bounty, and carried it away in bushel baskets. Everything happened so fast, I wondered if I had slipped into a dream. . . .

The day before, Daddy didn't join the men, even though we could'a used some coal. Doc James said Daddy had con-sump-shun. As cold as it was, I watched the sweat pour off his body, smelling up Mama's clean sheets. He looked a sight lying there—unmoving—in a cradle hole in the middle of the feather-ticked mattress, until a cough jolted him awake. The dark, wet spot in the bed grew larger; Daddy looked smaller.

In the night, his coughing woke up Audrey, my three-pound sister. Usually, she slept under his shirt on top of his chest next to his skin, his body heat keeping her alive.

My mother wanted to do more than nurse Audrey, but she couldn't. Doc James put Mama to bed, too, and warned her not to get up if she wanted to live. She had milk leg. It looked more like purple leg to me, all swole' up and ugly. With both Mama and Daddy down, I had to drop out of school.

"Flossie, is that you? Are you feeding Eloise?" Mama's call startled me.

"Yes, ma'am. She's eating again." I thought about my sisters: Audrey, barely a handful; Eloise, a year-old troublemaker; and Myrtle Lee, age four, ready to explore the world. I wondered how I got this job, but I knew. I was the big sister. Mama and Daddy depended on me.

The next morning, our world broke into more pieces than Eloise's bottle. Doc James and Mama talked in whispers. Finally, she told me Daddy had died in his sleep. Neighbor men came in and put him in a box that they set in the front room. I wondered what dead meant. Why didn't Daddy wake up?

Someone changed Audrey's handkerchief-sized diaper, placing her inside a handmade, pillowcase pocket that Mama had embroidered with flowers, then pinned it to the bed linens covering the bassinet mattress. Heated bricks wrapped in baby blankets surrounded the edge of the bed. That way, Audrey stayed warm enough.

When Mama's leg healed up, she went to work at the weaving mill on the late shift. I took care of all my sisters at night. Neither Mama nor I got enough rest during the day.

In the spring, Mama borrowed the neighbor's mule and wagon. She drove us to visit Daddy Jim, our granddaddy in the next county. When we arrived, his farm looked bigger than heaven itself—with row after row of corn, tomatoes and 'taters. Surely, it went on forever. My stomach griped. Inside, a lady seated us at a big table of food. I ate so much, I could hardly walk.

After dinner, Mama scooted me out in the yard to play with my cousins, but I sneaked around the house and watched her and Granddaddy through the window. As they talked, tears flowed down Mama's face like an underground stream just sprouted from a rock. Daddy Jim reached out for her, but she shook her head. "No, I won't have it!" she shouted, then stomped away.

I worried. Mama couldn't hide her swollen, red face. Soon, we headed for home. I grabbed Eloise and curled up as close as I could get to the front seat. "What's wrong, Mama?"

She stopped the wagon. "Flossie, I'll try to explain. You're still young, but you're my big girl now. You deserve to know the truth." She swallowed hard.

"Honey, we can't keep going on like this. I can't provide a decent life for you girls. You deserve a better place to live, and you need more than a third grade education, like your mama. I had hoped Daddy Jim would take in all you girls together and raise you right, but he says he can't. Oh, he's willing to split you up among relatives scattered over three counties, but I know you'd grow apart." Her jaw looked hard like Daddy's did the day he died. Then, she smiled. "I won't let that happen. I promise that I'll keep you girls together."

Weeks later, Mama packed us girls little bags of clothes and toys. We set out for the Mills Home Orphanage in Thomasville, North Carolina. Mama looked pale when she left us there that day, but she promised to visit as often as she could.

"This is for your own good," she said, stifling back tears.

Luckily, Mama's words came true. If we hadn't gone there when we did, two of my sisters would have died from tuberculosis. Perhaps none of us would have survived that old mill town at all. Instead, we girls lived in cottages right beside each other. The Mills Home nurtured us to become self-reliant, educated women. I didn't realize the magnitude of my mother's sacrifice—until I left, got married, and raised my own family.

As the last surviving sister at age ninety-two, I have cancer. It's the dead of winter, and my doctor says I'm gonna die very soon. But I've decided not to leave now when it's cold. I'll wait until the warm sun inspires early summer flowers to their glory.

Then, I'll go see Mama and be with her again. I'll thank her for the silk panties she sent me at Christmas, for every visit she made to the orphanage, and for putting us first in her life. She gave away us girls because she loved us so much, kind of like the sacrifice she said Jesus made for everyone.

I can see Mama smiling, waiting for me in heaven. I'll take her some flowers. . . .

Cinda Crawford

Jayne

Who so loves, believes the impossible.

Elizabeth Barret Browning

I told Jayne not to marry him. I agreed that he was very attractive and had lots of charm. He had a joyful demeanor that overlaid his more melancholic side—a unique and pleasant combination. There was no question that he was very intelligent and had a curiosity about all around him that kept him learning in a great variety of areas.

BUT I pointed out that she had just come out of a failed marriage and did not need to risk another one with a man she hardly knew whose prospects were at best questionable. He had dropped out of college and had spent the previous two years bumming around the country riding the rails and hitchhiking; had spent many an evening sitting around a camp fire with the bums along the railroad tracks as he traveled spontaneously from place to place. At this time it seemed that his health had been compromised by these two years of bumming. He had never held down a job for any length of time and had given no indication that he was ready to support a wife and child. In fact no indication of responsibility of any sort.

Fortunately our state at that time would not marry any one short of twenty-one years of age without a parental signature on a permission slip. I explained to her that feeling as I did there was no way I would sign a release for them to marry.

Did she accept my good advice? She did not. She listened graciously but responded, "I love him." I could see that she had already made up her mind and that nothing I might say would change it. They went ahead and planned their wedding for a few days after the twenty-first birthday.

I attended with a heavy heart seeing her darling pre-school son and wondering what was to become of them all. It didn't help me any to learn that the other parents, whom I met at the wedding for the first time, agreed heartily with my evaluation of the situation.

She was capable, loving, and always willing to give of herself; she did have a good job and a place to live; so I knew they would fare well enough financially but I had little hope that the marriage would last and didn't want her to have the responsibility of supporting not only her son from the previous marriage but also a second husband. It troubled me deeply to anticipate the pain that probably awaited Jayne after the first flush of joy had given way to the practical necessities of life.

Well the years went by. We kept in touch and things did seem to be going along very well. Her husband did get a job distributing newspapers and went back to college. After several years he graduated and moved on to a better job that required their moving to another state. I visited now and then but could not do so very often. The home they finally bought at their new location needed lots of fixing, which it turned out he was able and willing to do. I was encouraged to see this evidence of real responsibility and rejoiced to see Jayne's happiness in her marriage. I also noted that she patiently and lovingly supported him in all his endeavors. In fact I silently thought, *She is spoiling him too much.* But he did seem to thrive on it and showed tenderness toward her and her son whom he had adopted. I was both encouraged and pleased.

They now have three grown children and continue to be very happily married. Her love and generous spirit brought out all the best in him. She saw the depths and rich qualities of this man and had the faith to know these qualities would increase. I had only seen the youthful wanderlust and couldn't imagine, twenty-five years ago, that he would ever be the wonderful husband and father that he is to this day.

I now tell her often, "Thank you, Jayne. Thank you for marrying my son."

Frances Merwin

Bootsie

One can never creep when one feels an impulse to soar.

Helen Keller

Nobody has a mother who paints the outside of her house bright purple! And nobody has a mother named "Bootsie," who decorates the front yard with life-size mannequins and ceramic pigs costumed for every season and holiday. And certainly no one leaves her decorated purple Christmas tree up in the living room year-round! Nobody has a mother like that—except me! Therefore, I wasn't surprised at my friends' comments back in 1971 when I told them my mother was planning my wedding. "You've got to be kidding! A formal church wedding with 300 people and you are wearing a purple wedding dress?" "Where did you find a size 22 purple wedding dress?" "I can't believe that all ten members of the wedding party—including the men—are all wearing purple, too!"

Growing up in the 1950s in the small idyllic, conservative town of Clarksville, Missouri, I soon learned my mother was the antithesis of June Cleaver. My father's parents were graduates of the University of Missouri, class of 1919, and lived only two blocks away in a beautiful two-story brick home overlooking the Mississippi River. My grandfather was in the state legislature under Harry Truman, and my grandmother, whose mother had also graduated from college, was active in the DAR, Garden Club, and was a pillar of the Clarksville Christian Church. She was appalled when women began to wear pantsuits in public—much less shorts! Certainly, she had never met anyone like this boot-clad Memphis girl my father brought home as his bride after being stationed in Tennessee for basic training during WWII. I can only imagine what she must have thought of the purple house!

Raising a family in a town where everybody knew everybody—and all of their business—Bootsie didn't care if people said her shorts were too short, or her laugh too loud, or her boots out of fashion, or her house too purple. Both inside and out, for over five decades, the purple house has left visitors speechless. From steering wheels and flying pigs hanging from vaulted ceilings, to rooms of eclectic décor, one is mesmerized by multishaded purple shag carpeting not only on the floors but also occasional remnants randomly tossed onto newly painted, wet purple walls. My mother describes her sense of style as "unique." Her husband, children, grandchildren, and great-grandchildren certainly agree. She has taught us to be spontaneous, outgoing, and to live life to the fullest. Bootsie's unconditional love is reciprocated by all.

Only one person has caused my mother grief and pain through the years—me. As an adolescent, I somehow felt I needed to compete with Mom—and my beautiful older sister, Donna. They were my idols and my role models. Donna was beautiful and thin, just like Bootsie. She was a cheerleader, prom queen, valedictorian, and the daughter every mother wants. And I knew Bootsie was so proud of her. By fifteen I felt like an outcast; I quit trying to be like them. Instead, I turned to food and alcohol for comfort. At 250 pounds, I became rebellious and compensated in destructive ways unheard of back in the 1960s in Clarksville! I was regularly sent to the principal's office and suspended numerous times.

"Such a wonderful family except . . . poor Debbie." I heard that name so often that I lost count. But Bootsie always defended me and tried everything she humanly knew to help me. She fixed healthy food, purchased exercise equipment, and had my grandmother make my clothes when stores didn't have the plus sizes like today. She came to school numerous times on my behalf. I can still see her marching into the superintendent's office in her short shorts and boots to support "her baby girl," even when I was in the wrong. I learned how to manipulate and blame others for my problems—even Bootsie. It was easier than looking inside and facing my real issues. Yet she and Dad took me to counselors and psychiatrists and were always trying to rescue me from my abyss. But even Bootsie couldn't have prevented my attempted suicide.

One night I came home unexpectedly and found her all alone, doing something that I hadn't tried since I was a little girl; she was on her knees praying—for me. Call it a coincidence, but that moment impacted my future. As we began to talk, she told me of dreams she had given up so she could marry Dad during the war. She wasn't able to finish college, or become a fashion designer, or even to have the wedding she had always dreamed of. Instead, they were married in a little chapel—Dad in his Navy dress suit, and my mother in a plain blue suit—far from her childhood dreams! Until then, I had never known the young girl Bootsie; and I loved her even more.

With Mom's encouragement, I finally graduated from high school and met my future husband in college. Mom was thrilled to welcome her future son-in-law but was even more ecstatic when I asked her to plan my wedding as I finished my last semester of college. Since my sister Donna had eloped, my wedding became the "event" Bootsie had only been able to imagine!

Clarksville has never seen a wedding like mine—before or after. My hometown church had never been adorned with such an array of purple flowers, purple streamers and arches, and a five-tiered purple cake with a purple flowing fountain. In spite of the whispers and dropped jaws, I proudly floated down the aisle in my size-22 purple chiffon wedding dress, handmade by my grandmother. With the attendants in shades of purple and the men in purple tuxedoes, my matron of honor, Donna, said I looked just like our mother, Bootsie—who of course was the most outstanding beauty there! And she wasn't wearing boots!

Thirty-something years later, I have lost 100 pounds, and both my husband and I together can fit into the special wedding dress made by my grandmother. I became a high school drama teacher who had a built-in wardrobe for our plays— thanks to my mom, Bootsie. Her purple house was the first place I would look for costumes, props, and mannequins.

We recently took my parents to Europe to celebrate their sixtieth wedding anniversary; but they couldn't wait to get back to their purple house in Clarksville, Missouri! The purple Christmas tree is still decorated in July, children still want to see the pig collection, dreams are still being dreamed—and prayers are still being answered.

Dr. Debra Peppers

Blessings from Gran

It's faith in something and enthusiasm for something that makes a life worth living.

Oliver Wendell Holmes

At some point during my young adulthood, my grandmother was diagnosed with Alzheimer's. Leading up to this diagnosis, there had been many subtle changes in her behavior that were new and unfamiliar to me. More than ever before, I wanted to savor and treasure the "Gran" I knew and loved. The wisdom she shared was an accumulation of survival during the Depression, fifty years of marriage, and self-taught skills in a career as an editor's assistant. She had been uniquely helpful in the development of my writing skills and seemed to delight in proofreading my drafts. Over the next years, as the difficulties and challenges of Alzheimer's took its toll on my grandmother, an unexpected blessing found its way to me!

Throughout her life, Gran was extremely humble about her musical talent, but equally willing to share it with others. With few formal lessons, she had always considered her ability to play the piano a natural gift from

God, and she shared her faith in God through the hymns that she loved to play and sing so much. Many memories of family gatherings involve singing around the piano as our gran played. In fact, there is a part of me that chuckles whenever I think of her skillfully playing the old pump organ and singing until she was out of breath, getting her exercise for the day to boot!

In my childhood, I spent numerous hours building memories by Gran's side at the piano. Now, I was married and a mother myself. My children loved to sit with her at the piano as I had in my younger years. Even though her communication skills were disappearing, her patience with their young hands was predictable, and it thrilled me to watch her making memories with this next generation of her family.

Over the years following the diagnosis, her independence disappeared in most areas of her life, and her capabilities eventually paralleled a preschooler in many ways. Gran was moved to a nursing home a few miles from our home.

She could no longer speak in sentences, dress herself, or make decisions.

Whenever I went to visit, she and I would take a walk, and eventually end up at the piano in the activity room. As her other life skills deteriorated, I watched painfully anticipating that one day she would be unable to enjoy our visits to the piano. However, to my amazement and to the astonishment of the staff, God's gift graciously remained with her until the very last of her life. Her ability to sing and play the piano lingered as a treasured remnant of the capable person that she was in the past and the relationship shared between us over the years. Although there was barely a trace of her personality distinguishable at any other time, when she placed her fingers on the keys it was as if she was transformed from a vacant shell back into my beloved Gran.

As I brought my children to visit their great-grandmother in the nursing home, the time at the piano was always the highlight of our visits. Week after week we sat snuggled closely together on that piano bench in the activity room, allowing the words of the hymns that we sang in unison to be the communication that existed between us. Long after she was unable to call me by name, she was able to sing emphatically, with tears in her eyes and a passion in the words, "Make me a blessing to someone today."

Gran, without a doubt, you may be sure that you achieved that goal! Your blessing on my life and the faith heritage you shared with all your family continues to impact each one of us today!

Barbara Brown

8

SIMPLE TRUTHS, SOUND WISDOM

*What lies behind us and what lies before us
are tiny matters compared to what lies
within us!*

Ralph Waldo Emerson

Full Circle of Life

As a child, I failed to see
The woman right in front of me
Gave all she could . . . her heart and soul,
To teach me how to reach my goals.
And as I grew, my vision blurred,
Her words of wisdom were not heard.
I knew it all, she'd hear me say,
I couldn't wait to move away.
Adulthood came, I made mistakes.
She'd pick me up and soothe my aches,
And when, at times, I felt alone,
I'd find myself back at her home.
Now as a parent . . . frequently,
I repeat words she said to me,
I sound like her, we look the same,
I've come full circle in life's game.
Yes, through the years, her wisdom stayed,
Within my heart, it did not fade.
It just grew strong, and in the end,
My mom became my own best friend.

Cheryl Kremer

First Class Mother

People who say they sleep like a baby usually don't have one.

Leo J. Burke

The gentleman in seat 4A quickly stowed his overhead bag and settled into the plush leather seat in the first class cabin. Across the aisle, a fellow traveler was accepting a glass of champagne from the tall, slim flight attendant. The remaining seats were filling up quickly with middle-aged businessmen heading back to New York.

As I adjusted my seat belt, I sensed all eyes turning to the latest arrival to enter the first class cabin. A stunning, blond woman was checking her ticket for her seat assignment. All eyes watched her very closely. The man across from me held his breath.

When the woman stopped by seat 3B and made it clear she was not just passing through on her way to coach, the men looked horrified. Instead of being delighted to have this attractive woman as a seat companion, the men looked downright panicked.

What was the source of this palpable distress? The

woman's carry-on was not a stylish Louis Vuitton duffel bag; her *carry-on* was an infant seat containing a six-month-old baby . . . a baby who would be sharing the first class cabin with the business travelers for the long, five-hour flight. The men grumbled among themselves about the tiny trekker, who they were sure would start screaming any minute. Anticipating the imminent ordeal, one older, well-dressed gent went so far as to suggest there be a child-free section on every plane.

The mother settled her squirming daughter into her special safety seat and spoke to her in soothing tones. The plane reached its cruising altitude, a movie started, and the men reclined their leather seats and sipped their cocktails. As expected, it wasn't long before the darkened cabin was filled with noise . . . loud, unrelenting noise.

Standing up to head to the restroom, I caught the young mother's eye. Proceeding up the aisle, I gave her a sympathetic look as she tried to cover her ears to block out the incessant racket. With her baby sleeping peacefully at her side, the woman certainly looked as though she could use a nice, quiet opportunity to catch a much-needed nap . . . but the chorus of snoring sounds from the businessmen in the rows surrounding her and her baby was keeping her awake!

I paused by seat 3B. Sensing a kindred spirit, the woman leaned into the aisle and whispered conspiratorially, "Wouldn't it be wonderful if we had a quiet section on every plane just for mothers and babies?"

Pamela Hackett Hobson

Benedict Arnold Meets Barbie

Everything's got a moral, if only you can find it.

Lewis Carroll

To say I loved playing with Barbie dolls is an understatement akin to saying the Rockefellers are wealthy or the ocean is wide. I poured hours into playing with my Barbies—changing clothes, combing hair, rolling the Corvette down the driveway, operating the elevator in the three-story town house. I had multiple dolls that answered to "Barbie," as well as Midge, Skipper, and two Kens. Most had the long, straight blond hair and perfectly tanned skin of the 1970s ideal California girl, but I also had one of an earlier era with a short, dark pageboy haircut, puckered lips, and eye makeup that looked like Elizabeth Taylor in Cleopatra. I had the Growing Up Skipper doll— the one that, with a few twists of her arm, transformed from a flat-chested little girl to a budding-breast adolescent. It's a wonder all the little girls of 1976 didn't do permanent damage to their shoulders trying to attempt the same feat.

When I wasn't playing with them, I kept my dolls in a large suitcase. It was a piece from the first set of luggage my mother ever owned, round and gray, a style not seen any more. The cavern in the center was full of clothes, and the large pocket in the lid was where I kept the dolls. The shirred pockets around the inside of the case held all the small accessories—shoes, purses, tiny household appliances.

As I entered sixth grade, my Barbie passion began to wane. The suitcase remained unopened, the town house uninhabited, the pool empty, the Corvette up on metaphorical blocks. Maybe it's because I got a TV in my room, maybe because you can only twist a doll's arm so many times before becoming overwhelmed by the inadequacy of your own body. Whatever the reason, I lived for many oblivious months, paying no attention to the years' worth of Barbie bounty gathered in my closet.

Until I came home from school one day and it was all gone.

"Mom!" I screamed, over and over again, running through the house until I finally found her. "Mom! All my Barbie stuff is gone!"

"I know," she replied calmly.

"Where is it?"

"I gave it away."

Struck dumb by the betrayal, I stared at her. Then, hoping there was some sort of misunderstanding, I ran back to my room.

But it was all gone. The purple go-go boots. The fur-lined parka. The bicycle I could never position the dolls' legs on properly. The modest house where my Sunshine Family lived as Barbie's less glamorous neighbors. Squishy-head Ken; hard-head Ken. The Jeep.

Mom stood in my bedroom doorway. There were no words for the emptiness I felt. So I just cried, sitting there in the now-empty space, and still more when my mother sat on my bed and took me in her arms.

"There's a family on Post that adopted two little girls from Vietnam," my mother explained. "These little girls have nothing. No family. No toys. Imagine if you had to go live far away in some strange place and you had nothing."

"I do have nothing, now," I sniffled into my mother's warm lap.

"No, Allison. You have all kinds of things. You haven't played with these toys in months."

"But they were mine," I said. "You didn't even ask me."

My mother paused there for a minute. Then she said, "You're right. I assumed you wouldn't mind because you never played with them anymore. If it means that much to you, I'll call the family and see if we can get them back."

But even I, as selfish and self-centered as I could be, knew that you just didn't go to orphaned children from a war-torn country and take your toys back. Besides, I considered it much more important to have this little act of treason as something to hold over my mother's head for years to come. Whenever we got into the inevitable clashes that will come when two women—one established and one emerging—share a house, I would bring up the fact that my mother had scarred me in ways unimaginable. That I had trouble trusting authority figures. That I still had some compulsive need to inspect the corners of my room to be sure she hadn't traded away a favorite sweater I hadn't worn since the previous winter, or abandon the cat I forgot to feed.

More than twenty years after the great Barbie betrayal of 1977, I was teaching Junior English at a high school in Texas. My students had an assignment to write about an important childhood memory. One lovely girl I'll call Annie titled her essay "My First Barbie." The child of a poor Vietnamese woman and an American soldier, Annie had been given over to one set of relatives after another, before finally being adopted by an American family. She arrived in this country when she was five years old, terrified and alone. She spoke no English, had no real idea of what was happening to her, but when she went into her new bedroom, she saw a basketful of Barbie dolls in the corner, and when she met some other little girls in her neighborhood, she saw that they had the same dolls she did, and she knew how to play. "That," she wrote, "was the first time I ever felt at home."

The day I read that essay was the day I forgave my mother. Later, I called and begged her to forgive me for ever doubting her generosity and kindness. The bitterness I'd held on to for so long dissolved into a profound respect for my mother when I realized that, had she asked, I would have refused, and she would have respected my wishes. How blessed I am to have a mother with the wisdom to allow me to do something good against my own wishes. I thank God that somewhere, two grown women —strangers to me—share my blessing as much as they shared my Barbies.

Allison Pittman

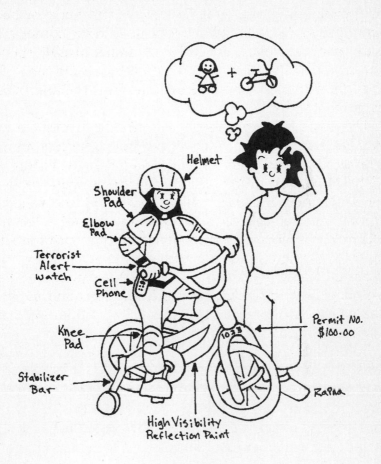

Reprinted by permission of Robert. C. Raina. ©*2006 Robert C. Raina.*

Retrospect

Making the decision to have a child—it's momentous. It is to decide forever to have your heart go walking outside your body.

Elizabeth Stone

Today, I left the small fingerprints on the windowpane. I left the toy in the corner, and the dishes undone. I rocked her extra long as she lay peacefully on my breast.

Today, I held her hand as we walked the soon-to-be familiar path to her first day at school. She smiled and waved good-bye. She didn't see the tear in my eye or feel the lump in my throat. Later, I showed her the way home and listened to every little thing that excited her heart.

Today she met her first young love. He held her hand in his while his eyes spoke a thousand words of love. His future intertwined with hers as their hearts beat as one. I shared her joy. She couldn't see the tear in my eye or feel the lump in my throat.

Today was her day. A cap, a gown, a tassel! A celebration of all she had become and all she had to offer. A day of promise, new beginnings, and dreams. Where had my little girl gone? I wanted to hold her against my breast and rock her extra long.

Today was their day. The white gown, the music, the roses, the lilies, and the love. I let go of her hand. Yet, my arms remained open. This day of joy! She didn't see the tear in my eye or feel the lump in my throat.

Today was our day. God's gift to them. Their gift to each other. Their gift to us. So small, so sleepy, so perfect, so beautiful. I took her in my arms. Her little fingers curled around mine. I was older now—a grandmother! I held her against my breast and rocked her extra long.

Today was my day. She held me against her breast and rocked me extra long. I had left fingerprints in her life. She listened as I told her of my pain. Today, she was there to help me home. Today, I couldn't see the tear in her eye or feel the lump in her throat.

Today, she placed a rose in my hand. She remembered the fragrance of life and the bond we shared. Today, she placed a white lily on my grave while she held a small hand in hers.

Today, she held her against her breast and rocked her extra long. God saw the tears in their eyes and felt the lumps in their throats. He wrapped his loving arms around them and rocked them extra long.

Glorianne M. Swenson

Walking Lessons

Walking, I learned, is a kind of a prayer, the body swinging along at a steady rhythm as the legs and feet dance onwards and the soul is released.

Michele Roberts

I am just back from a walk. My muddy sneakers are drying near the back door, not far from my damp raincoat. Tiny, the dog, has curled up to rest in her corner of the couch. Tommy, the husband, is checking the answering machine. The world is leaving us alone for this chilly spring Sunday afternoon, and that is fine with me as I make the tea and reflect on the souvenirs from the three miles we've just covered. Tommy enthusing about a new CD, Tiny discovering a deer bone in a field, a smaller bird giving warning to a circling hawk, the river finally slowing and lowering after raging winter highs. I wonder how different it might look tomorrow, because I'll be back then. And the day after that, and the day after that.

Walking is a part of most of my days. Not because of some recent fitness craze but as a natural practice since toddlerhood, when my mother gave me that lesson.

The way I see it, she taught me to walk twice.

The first time was the usual way chronicled in so many snapshot albums. A tot stumbling forward, arms raised to connect with unseen hands that are steadying posture and gait, gently guiding the way as a voice encourages: "This way, that's right, good for you."

And while those lessons were so crucial to the blessing of mobility, I don't even give a thought to them as I move through my day; my other walking lessons are ones I reflect on often, as I cross fields, trace riverbanks, cover city blocks. Because after my mother taught me to actually walk, she went on to teach me how to get somewhere with great enjoyment of weather, scenery, and the simple process of movement.

The lengthy and frequent walks that filled my childhood weren't just to the end of the street. No simple stroll to the post office on level sidewalks. Even back when my older sister and I weren't yet in first grade, my mother took us to the highest points in our little New England village. Up the challenging half-paved grade of the wonderfully named Baptist Hill. Down the lengthy and winding Corn Road, which must have had another name but was given that one by us because of the fields of butter-and-sugar that lined the route.

My mother would pack a plaid vinyl cooler with a Thermos of milk and peanut butter and jelly sandwiches, and she, Mary Ann, and I would set off for distant lands. At least the destinations seemed that far as we crossed bridges, passed farmland, entered woods. I'm sure we talked along the way, pointing out butterflies or the church steeple sticking from the treetops, but better than any conversation, I remember the stories in my head. (I write for a living and even as a tiny kid made things up from the reality I was in.) As we scaled hills in my mother's footsteps, I turned us into pioneers searching for a place to make our home. Walking along a sunbaked patch of road, staring down at our trio of moving shadows, I pretended that the Thermos was our only source of water for weeks. Passing through woods, I conjured that we were in search of a magical land no one had ever seen before— but we would find it! My favorite destination was a van-sized rock that jutted from the woods like the prow of a boat. We'd climb that final few feet and sit to enjoy the view of our valley and the spread of basic sandwich and drink that tasted better than anything we'd ever been served. There was a satisfaction I still feel at the conclusion of a walk: that I got myself somewhere. Under my own power.

My mother was giving me what would become my sport, if you will. I can't throw a ball anywhere predictable, running makes me feel ill, but give me my sneakers and point me in a direction and I'm gone, throwing one leg in front of the other, rolling from heel to toe, speeding along. Through the forest, along the river, up some of those same hills my mother led us when she unknowingly inspired what would become my daily practice, one that has me setting out wherever I find myself: be that up a Colorado hillside like one morning last weekend, delighted at the discovery of an actual cactus in my path; tracing the edge of an Irish peninsula for eight spring days a few years ago; or back home this afternoon, checking the height of that river. No matter the setting, there is the same thrill of movement, energy, breath, and a soul-renewing, mind-clearing, ever-changing scene; there is that simple and treasured gift from mother to child.

There are no phone messages today from anyone, but I decide to make a call. I dial my mother on this gray damp Sunday afternoon.

"What's new?" she asks.

"I just came back from a walk."

"Good for you," she says.

And I agree.

Suzanne Strempek Shea

Learning Curve

Children are likely to live up to what you believe of them.

Lady Bird Johnson

"I want this one!" Holly, one of my five-year-old twin daughters yells, snatching from the wicker basket a plastic egg speckled with gold glitter.

"No fair!" her sister wails. "That's the best one! I want it, too!"

I'm not even sure where the coveted glitter egg came from, but I should have known it would cause a ruckus. There is, after all, only one gold-speckled glitter egg, and two five-year-old glitter-crazy girls. I think about taking it out of the egg hunt completely and placing it on top of the refrigerator where all banished desirables collect dust when squabbles break out in our house. But in the ensuing chaos, it is left in the basket, hidden with its other less-flashy, less-desirable brethren.

Holly, her glitter-homing senses sharpened to perfection, finds the egg first. I watch from across the yard as she picks it up and holds it aloft triumphantly. It's as if she's found the Holy Grail. She is inordinately excited. I groan. At this point I know just what will happen next. Holly will run right over to her sister and taunt, "Ha, ha, ha! Look what I found! I got the best one!" right in Brittany's face, and then there will crying and whining and something that was supposed to be fun will be ruined over a silly plastic glitter egg. I can feel my blood pressure rising. I open my mouth to warn my daughter not to go there and kick myself for not removing the egg.

She races by me, her prize clutched tightly to her chest. Her face is radiant. "Holly!" I say sternly.

She turns and realizes I am there. She looks taken aback by my tone, but her enthusiasm is unquenched. "Look, Mommy, look what I found! I found the best egg. Where's Brittany?"

Oh, how well I know five-year-olds, I think. I can practically read her mind. "Don't you dare . . ." I say. But my daughter is not listening. She keeps running. Her words trail behind her.

"I have to find Brittany, Mom! This is the egg she wanted, and I found it for her. She's going to love this!"

I bite off my words and swallow shame. Watching my daughters revel in glitter-induced ecstasy, sharing candies and laughing, I think of all the times I know the answers based on what I see before me. Of all the times I'm ready to teach someone a lesson, only to find out that the only person behind the learning curve is me. I stand and watch a five-year-old alchemist transform plastic into true treasure. And I think, not for the first time, how very good it is to be wrong.

Karen Crafts Driscoll

"Grandma, how can I put one of
your hugs in my scrapbook?"

Wings to Fly

The world is round and the place which may seem like the end may also be the beginning.

Ivy Baker Priest

"Mom, Ed's here. Now, be cool, just take our pictures and we're leaving. And, Dad, don't ask Ed a lot of questions. He's a good guy, and I promise not to stay out all night," Jen said.

With that, the stage was set for the Junior Prom. The handsome young man posed with my sixteen-year-old daughter, who had a corsage on her wrist and the look of love in her eyes.

This was my special daughter whom I cried over when I found out I was pregnant just two months after her brother's birth. I thought I wasn't ready for another child so soon. Then this blond baby girl arrived with blue eyes as big as saucers and stole my heart. Funny how, from the day of her complicated delivery, we forged a bond tighter than superglue. We could finish each other's sentences, knew with a glance when the other was hurting, and kidded each other that it was too bad we were related because we'd make perfect soul mates.

Jen and Ed dated throughout high school and married a year after graduation. Jen lived in an apartment about a mile from us while Ed was in Navy boot camp. We shopped together on Saturdays and went to church as a family on Sundays. She often joined us for dinner, the same as she did before she was married, so nothing seemed like it had changed.

Eventually, Ed came home and the happy couple moved an hour away from us to San Diego where his Navy base was located. Soon one child and then another joined them, they bought a house, and became a family. I missed Jen, but we spent holidays with her and Ed, and lots of weekends in between.

One night the phone rang. "Mom, get Dad on the extension, I have big news for you both." I called my husband and while he listened in, Jen explained in an excited breath, "We're being transferred to Japan for three years; isn't that exciting?"

My heart gave a jump; I stared numbly at the phone. *Japan! That's so far away,* I thought. *It's halfway around the world; how will we see each other?*

"That's great," I mumbled. The rest of the conversation has left my memory. I was devastated.

In Atsugi, Jen insisted they live off the base so they could experience the full cultural immersion. She learned to drive on the opposite side of the road and take the bullet train to Tokyo alone. She found some Japanese women who longed to learn English. Jen taught them English, and they taught her Japanese. Each week they enjoyed one another's company and ended the lessons with a cup of sake. She learned to cook yakisoba and drink tea instead of soda pop. She even learned how to do the traditional Japanese tea ceremony. In short, she reveled in the culture.

Jen thrived in Japan, and something else happened; she

became an independent woman. With Ed out to sea a lot, she became the single mother, nursemaid, disciplinarian, and homework tutor.

Meanwhile, back home, I lived for our Sunday night phone calls when I could get through on the busy circuits. E-mails became precious; photos in the mail were like holiday gifts.

One Saturday, I was at my friend's house for coffee.

"Oh, Erika, I miss Jen so much my heart aches. I don't understand how my daughter ended up halfway around the world. One minute she was here and then she was gone. Just like a bird, she flew away."

Erika took my hand in hers. "Sallie, you raised her to be all she could be, to revel in life, and be her own person, right?"

I nodded.

"Well, she may have flown away just like a bird, but remember, it is because you gave her the wings to fly."

Sallie A. Rodman

To a Daughter . . .

If I kept you too close, it was because you were such a joy
to be near.
If I embarrassed you by bragging about you too much, it
was because I was so proud of the person you are.
If I pushed too hard or expected too much, it was because
I knew you were capable of great things.
If I didn't give you as much freedom as I should have, it
was because I wanted to protect you from those whom
your innocent heart didn't realize would harm you.
If I didn't let you be "you," then that was just plain wrong
because "you" are a "masterpiece."
And if I'm still holding on too tightly, it is because letting
you go is so hard.

Tonna Canfield

More Chicken Soup?

We would love to hear your reactions to the stories in this book. Please let us know what your favorite stories were and how they affected you.

Many of the stories and poems you have read in this book were submitted by readers like you who had read earlier Chicken Soup for the Soul books. We publish many Chicken Soup for the Soul books every year. We invite you to contribute a story to one of these future volumes.

Stories may be up to 1,200 words and must uplift or inspire. You may submit an original piece, something you have read or your favorite quotation on your refrigerator door.

To obtain a copy of our submission guidelines and a listing of upcoming *Chicken Soup* books, please write, fax, or check our websites. Please send your submissions to:

website: www.chickensoup.com
Chicken Soup for the Soul
P.O. Box 30880 • Santa Barbara, CA 93130
fax: 805-563-2945

Just send a copy of your stories and other pieces to the above address. We will be sure that both you and the author are credited for your submission.

For information about speaking engagements, other books, audiotapes, workshops, and training programs, please contact any of our authors directly.

Supporting Others

The authors of this book are deeply appreciative of the opportunity to share a portion of the proceeds with an organization whose mission over many years has been to help individuals and our world. This organization continues its commitment to mothers and daughters through workshops, trainings, and groups.

The Synthesis Center

The Synthesis Center is a nonprofit educational organization in Amherst, Massachusetts. The goal of the Center is to have a positive impact in the world through offering psychosynthesis counselor training, community counseling, workshops, and educational programs. Psychosynthesis is a spiritually oriented psychology whose assumptions support a view of the basic goodness of people, the promise of meaningful and purposeful lives, and the power of individuals, families, and communities to make change in themselves and in their world. It is the hope and the day-to-day work of all of the people at the center that they may help create peace and health, in every person and in the world. The center is committed to offering low-cost services to those in need.

The Synthesis Center is the home of the first mother/daughter workshops run by the Firmans. It continues to support the well-being of mothers and daughters through all of its programs. For more information on the center, visit their website at www.synthesiscenter.org. To sign up for the center's electronic newsletter or to be on the mailing list, or to contact the Firmans, write or call:

The Synthesis Center
274 North Pleasant Street
Amherst, MA 01002
413-256-0772

Who Is Jack Canfield?

Jack Canfield is the cocreator and editor of the Chicken Soup for the Soul series, which *Time* magazine has called "the publishing phenomenon of the decade." The series now has 105 titles with over 100 million copies in print in forty-one languages. Jack is also the coauthor of eight other bestselling books including *The Success Principles: How to Get from Where You Are to Where You Want to Be*, *Dare to Win*, *The Aladdin Factor*, *You've Got to Read This Book*, and *The Power of Focus: How to Hit Your Business and Personal and Financial Targets with Absolute Certainty.*

Jack has recently developed a telephone coaching program and an online coaching program based on his most recent book *The Success Principles*. He also offers a seven-day Breakthrough to Success seminar every summer, which attracts 400 people from fifteen countries around the world.

Jack has conducted intensive personal and professional development seminars on the principles of success for over 900,000 people in twenty-one countries around the world. He has spoken to hundreds of thousands of others at numerous conferences and conventions and has been seen by millions of viewers on national television shows such as *The Today Show, Fox and Friends, Inside Edition, Hard Copy, CNN's Talk Back Live, 20/20, Eye to Eye,* the *NBC Nightly News,* and the *CBS Evening News.*

Jack is the recipient of many awards and honors, including three honorary doctorates and a Guinness World Records Certificate for having seven books from the Chicken Soup for the Soul series appearing on the *New York Times* bestseller list on May 24, 1998.

To write to Jack or for inquiries about Jack as a speaker, his coaching programs, or his seminars, use the following contact information:

The Canfield Companies
P.O. Box 30880 • Santa Barbara, CA 93130
phone: 805-563-2935 • fax: 805-563-2945
E-mail: info@jackcanfield.com or
visit his website at www.jackcanfield.com

Who Is Mark Victor Hansen?

In the area of human potential, no one is more respected than Mark Victor Hansen. For more than thirty years, Mark has focused solely on helping people from all walks of life reshape their personal vision of what's possible. His powerful messages of possibility, opportunity, and action have created powerful change in thousands of organizations and millions of individuals worldwide.

He is a sought-after keynote speaker, bestselling author, and marketing maven. Mark's credentials include a lifetime of entrepreneurial success and an extensive academic background. He is a prolific writer with many bestselling books, such as *The One Minute Millionaire, Cracking the Millionaire Code, How to Make the Rest of Your Life the Best of Your Life, The Power of Focus, The Aladdin Factor,* and *Dare to Win,* in addition to the *Chicken Soup for the Soul* series. Mark has made a profound influence through his library of audios, videos, and articles in the areas of big thinking, sales achievement, wealth building, publishing success, and personal and professional development.

Mark is the founder of the MEGA Seminar Series. MEGA Book Marketing University and Building Your MEGA Speaking Empire are annual conferences where Mark coaches and teaches new and aspiring authors, speakers, and experts on building lucrative publishing and speaking careers. Other MEGA events include MEGA Info-Marketing and My MEGA Life.

As a philanthropist and humanitarian, Mark works tirelessly for organizations such as Habitat for Humanity, American Red Cross, March of Dimes, Childhelp USA, and many others. He is the recipient of numerous awards that honor his entrepreneurial spirit, philanthropic heart, and business acumen. He is a lifetime member of the Horatio Alger Association of Distinguished Americans, an organization that honored Mark with the prestigious Horatio Alger Award for his extraordinary life achievements.

Mark Victor Hansen is an enthusiastic crusader of what's possible and is driven to make the world a better place.

Mark Victor Hansen & Associates, Inc.
P.O. Box 7665 • Newport Beach, CA 92658
phone: 949-764-2640 • fax: 949-722-6912
www.markvictorhansen.com

Who Is Dorothy Firman?

Dr. Dorothy Firman is a professor at Union Institute and University of Vermont College Counseling and Psychology Graduate program. She is also a psychotherapist, life coach, author, consultant, speaker, and trainer. She has worked in the field of mother and daughter relationships for more than twenty-five years, offering workshops, seminars, and key-note presentations with her mother, Julie. Their book, *Daughters and Mothers, Making It Work,* now in its fifth printing, is designed as an active workbook for women wanting to become whole in relationships and in themselves.

Dorothy is a founding member of the Association for the Advancement of Psychosynthesis, a spiritual psychology that she first encountered in her early years as a student and colleague of Jack Canfield. For twenty-five years, Dorothy has been a trainer of helping professionals in the field of psychosynthesis, offering people the opportunity to deepen their experience of aliveness, presence, and the ability to serve. Her training is run through The Synthesis Center, a nonprofit educational organization cofounded by Jack Canfield in 1976.

Dorothy has three adult children, each a unique and amazing soul, and two incredible granddaughters. She has been married to her best friend for thirty years. As the children left home, Dorothy took the opportunity to become a potter and a martial artist. In both of these worlds, she relishes her beginner's status, being the student and not the teacher.

For more information, contact Dr. Firman at:

285 Pomeroy Lane
Amherst, MA 01002
Phone: 413-256-3020
Websites: DFirman@comcast.net
www.synthesiscenter.org
www.motherdaughterrelations.com

Who Is Julie Firman?

Julie Firman is the mother of two daughters—her coauthors—and one son. She has eight grandchildren and two great-granddaughters. She has been married to her wonderful husband for sixty-five years. Julie has had a range of careers from school teacher and school administrator to psychotherapist, group leader, trainer, author, and speaker. She and her daughter, Dorothy, are the authors of *Daughters and Mothers, Making It Work* and have led workshops on the mother-daughter relationship at numerous conferences and centers around the country.

At eighty-seven, Julie doesn't play tennis several times a week like her husband, but she is still very active in the community. Part of her legacy will always be "Rehearsal Dinner Queen" because she has hosted a large rehearsal dinner for three different grandchildren, creating a wonderful family tradition. The grandchildren visit from all over North America, and the family gathers at Julie and Win's for one of their big dinner parties.

Julie has recently retired from her formal "mother-daughter" work, but she still speaks occasionally to local groups and continues to write to and consult mothers and daughters in *kitchen table* fashion. You can email her at Juliefirm@aol.com.

Who Is Frances Firman Salorio?

Frances Firman Salorio is a solution-focused marriage and family therapist. She began her work in this field at the Christian Counseling Center in Norwalk, Connecticut, almost twenty years ago. There have been other jobs and other locations in the intervening years, but she always returns to work with this wonderful group of people who see individuals, couples, and families and help them with a wide variety of life issues.

Frances now lives in Amherst, Massachusetts, not far from her parents and her sister. It's fulfilling to be in close contact with family and to be able to enjoy time with older parents on a regular basis. She travels to visit her terrific children in Maryland and Alberta, far-flung but in close touch. These two adult children (and a very special daughter-in-law) make life interesting and meaningful. When they all visit Amherst and the extended local family gets together, life couldn't be better.

Luckily, the new home in Amherst isn't far from the old home in New York, so Frances has not had to give up her book group of more than thirty years. Seeing long-time friends and enjoying intellectual pursuits are monthly highlights (along with two other local book groups). Add swimming to the mix, along with the nieces and nephews who come to the pool in the summer, and life is very rewarding.

Frances says that, as with being a therapist, the experience of working with many authors and hearing their stories and sharing their highs and lows has added depth and learning to life. This second Chicken Soup book has been as rewarding as the first. You can contact Frances at fsalorio@comcast.net.

Contributors

The stories in this book are original pieces or taken from previously published sources, such as books, magazines, and newspapers. If you would like to contact any of the contributors for information about their writing or would like to invite them to speak in your community, look for their contact information included in their biography.

Jessica Adam enjoys many hobbies. But with four children and a career, finding time is always a challenge. She has long dreamed of being a published writer so one hobby she always makes time for is writing in her journal. You can e-mail her at meggiehca@yahoo.com.

Nancy Baker resides in College Station, Texas, with her husband and golden retriever. When she retired from the university where she worked as a program coodinator, she pursued her love of writing and has been published in numerous anthologies and magazines, including *Chicken Soup for the Christian Soul II*.

As president of Open Mind Adventures, **Aimee Bernstein** guides individuals in transforming their lives, their organizations, and their communities. Aimee is a psychotherapist with thirty years of experience, a teacher of energy awareness principles, and an internationally acclaimed speaker. Currently she is exploring the field of geriatrics as it relates to the psychological and spiritual needs of caretakers. Aimee can be contacted at aimeeoma1@bellsotuh.net.

Marilyn Bodwell has enjoyed writing and oil painting for many years. She is a professional artist living in Mirror Lake, New Hampshire. Her first grandchild, Patrick, has been followed by seven more, most recently twin grandsons born June 2006. She was a former TWA flight attendant, and tennis player. Her surroundings are her inspirations—deer, moose, bears, bald eagles, and her favorite, the loons.

Carolyn Brooks is a speaker, author, Bible teacher, and corporate consultant. Her books include *Conversations on Faith, But Lord I Was Happy Shallow,* and *What I Learned From God While Cooking.* Her new book releases are *Breaking the Silent Addiction of Abuse, America's Genocide Exposed,* and *Moving Up the Corporate Ladder God's Way.* Visit her at www.carolynbrooks.com.

Barbara Brown, native of Nashville, Tennessee, is a Registered Nurse at Vanderbilt. She and husband, Jim have five children and are grandparents to three little boys. This story is dedicated to Margaret Brock, Barbara's maternal grandmother, who died in 1994 after a long battle with Alzheimer's.

Martha Campbell is a graduate of Washington University, St. Louis School of Fine Arts, and a former writer and designer for Hallmark Cards. She has been a freelance cartoonist and book illustrator since 1973. She can be reached at P.O. Box 2538 Harrison, Arizona, or at marthaf@alltel.net.

Tonna Canfield lives in Ashland, Kentucky, with her husband, Jeff. They have two daughters, Natalie and Erica. Tonna was a contributor to the first *Chicken Soup for the Mother & Daughter Soul* Book. She also has had stories published in *God's Way for Graduates.*

David Cooney's cartoons and illustrations have appeared in numerous *Chicken Soup for the Soul* books as well as magazines, including *USA Weekend* and *Good Housekeeping.* David lives with his wife, Marcia, and two children, Sarah and Andrew, in the small Pennsylvania town of Mifflinburg. His website is www.DavidCooney.com and he can be reached at david@davidcooney.com.

Cinda Crawford loves to write Christian suspense fiction. Her latest work, *From the Floor Looking Up,* is a memoir/inspirational health book that details how she recovered from chronic fatigue syndrome, fibromyalgia, and other chronic illnesses. Cinda's life-changing story offers hope and help to millions of people. You can visit her website at www.cindacrawford.com.

Kelly Curtis is an author, speaker, former guidance counselor, and founder of Empowering Youth, Inc. She writes about youth-related topics and speaks throughout the United States about issues related to youth empowerment and Developmental Assets. Kelly enjoys traveling, writing, and spending time with her family. You can contact Kelly at www.kellycurtis.com.

Susan Rothrock Deo is an author of children's books and teaches science at a southern California college. As a volunteer she also shares the wonders of nature with children of all ages. She and her husband have two daughters who are the joy of their lives. You can contact Susan at susan.deo@gmail.com.

Mary Dixon Lebeau (marylebeau@comcast.net) is a writer, counselor, wife, and mother of five. Her work has appeared in such publications as *Family Circle, AARP, Parenting,* and two previous editions of *Chicken Soup.* Mary is still inspired by her mother and misses her every day—especially in October.

Amanda Dodson and her best friend and mother, Patsy Thornhill began a trendy pet line, Fifi & Fido (Fififido.com), in 2004. Their products can be found in gift stores nationwide and have been featured in magazines and national media. When she isn't working side by side with her mother, she continues to do occasional freelance writing. Her biggest accomplishment to date is the blessing of raising her two children, Gracie and Garrett.

Karen Crafts Driscoll lives with her husband and their four children in Connecticut.

Sara Elinoff-Acker still finds it amazing that she became a mother at age forty-three. Although she can't stay awake past 9 PM, midlife motherhood is the greatest adventure of her life. She is the director of a domestic violence intervention program and is writing a book about recovered abusers. She lives in Western Massachusetts.

Author, poet, freelance writer, and columnist, **M. Mylene English** delivers her sometimes quirky, sometimes cheeky views with honesty and humor in her newspaper column *It'll Be Fine,* which has appeared regularly in northern Alberta newspapers since 1992. Mylene also currently writes for *Canadian Scrapbooker* magazine. She lives in northern Alberta with her husband and five children who provide continual support of (and inspiration for) her writing. For more of her work, including books, cards, and photography, please visit www.echoecho.ca. Contact can be made through wordsmith@echoecho.ca.

Carol Ann Erhardt is a published author with The Wild Rose Press. She lives in Columbus, Ohio, with her husband Ron and three resident cats—Charlotte,

Wilbur, and Templeton. She is an avid reader and a passionate writer. Contact Carol Ann at cae@carolannerhardt.com or visit www.carolannerhardt.com.

Debbie Farmer writes the award-winning syndicated column "Family Daze." Her book, *Don't Put Lipstick on the Cat*, is available online or in bookstores. When not busy writing or being a mom, Debbie is either teaching first grade, shopping for shoes, or meeting friends for coffee. For information on having "Family Daze" appear in your newspaper, you can e-mail familydaze@home.com, or visit the "Family Daze" website at www.familydaze.com.

Margaret S. Frezon is a writer from upstate New York and a frequent contributor to *Guideposts, Sweet 16, Angels on Earth, Positive Thinking*, and *Chicken Soup* books. She is currently working on a novel about stepping into adulthood, inspired by her daughter. You can contact Peggy at ecritMeg@nycap.rr.com.

Sally Friedman, a frequent contributor to the *Chicken Soup* series, has been writing personal essays for three decades. Her work has appeared in the *New York Times, Family Circle, Brides*, and *Ladies Home Journal*. Her best work, she insists, is motherhood. You can contact her at pinegander@aol.com.

Jennifer Gramigna, now residing in New York with her husband and three children, was raised in Cincinnati, Ohio, the youngest of seven (and then fourteen) siblings. After graduating cum laude from Long Island University in 1979, she works in theatre, film, TV, and radio.

Pamela Hackett Hobson is the author of two novels—*The Bronxville Book Club* and *The Silent Auction*. Pam's debut novel, *The Bronxville Book Club*, was featured in the *New York Times*. To learn more about the author and her writing projects, visit www.pamelahobson.com or send an e-mail to author@pamelahobson.com.

Heather Halderman began writing seven years ago after her oldest son left for college. She has been married to her husband, Hank, for twenty-seven years and has three children. She has published several personal essays and is currently writing a book. She can be reached at Heathheh2ao.com.

Cynthia Hamond has numerous stories in the *Chicken Soup for the Soul* series, *Multnomah's Stories for the Heart*, major publications, including *Woman's World* magazine and *King Features Syndicate*. She received two writing awards and was a featured author on *Anthology Today*. *Goodwill* and *Friends to the End* are her favorite TV programs. You can visit Cynthia's website at CynthiaHamond.com.

Christie A. Hansen has three children and a bachelor degree in English from Utah State University. She wrote a weekly parenting column for three years and is currently seeking a literary agent interested in representing children's books and inspirational nonfiction for women. Her musings can be found online at www.bellyacrefarm.blogspot.com.

Jonny Hawkins, from Sherwood Michigan, is a twenty-year cartoonist whose work has appeared in over 350 publications. His books and calendars—such as *Medical Cartoons-A-Day, Fishing Cartoons-A-Day*, and *Cartoons for Teachers* are available in bookstores and online. He can be reached at jonnyhawkins2nz@yahoo.com.

Eve Eschner Hogan is an inspirational speaker and the author of several books, including *How to Love Your Marriage, Intellectual Foreplay*, and *Way of the Winding Path*. She was the senior editor for *Chicken Soup for the African American Soul* and *Chicken Soup for the African American Woman's Soul*. You can visit Eve's website at www.EveHogan.com, or contact her at Eve@HeartPath.com.

Georgia A. Hubley retired after twenty years in financial management to write her memoirs. She's a frequent contributor to the *Chicken Soup for the Soul* series and numerous national magazines and newspapers. She has two grown sons and resides with her husband in Henderson, Nevada. You can contact her at GEOHUB@aol.com.

Armené Humber is a career coach and writer whose stories have appeared in numerous publications. She has a master's degree in Christian Leadership from Fuller Theological Seminary, lives with her husband in Southern California, and feels privileged to serve people who are courageously struggling with unemployment. You can contact her at armhumber@aol.com.

Annette M. Irby enjoys writing songs, articles, and novels. Born in Michigan, she now resides near Seattle, Washington, with her husband and three children. Her work has appeared in various journals and devotionals. Currently she is writing a trilogy and pursuing publication of that series as well as two novels.

Mimi Greenwood Knight is a freelance writer and artist. Her current residence is in what's left of South Louisiana where she lives with her husband, David, four kids, four dogs, four cats, and one obnoxious bird. Her parenting essays and articles have appeared in *Parents Magazine, American Baby, Working Mother, Christian Parenting Today, Today's Christian Woman,* and in anthologies, including several *Chicken Soup* books.

Helene Kopel is a single mom living with her ten-year-old daughter just outside of Ft. Lauderdale, Florida. She currently works as an E-commerce Manager for a direct mail company and an Online Marketing Consultant for other business to business companies.

Cheryl Kremer lives in Lancaster, Pennsylvania, with her husband, Jack, and her two kids: Nikki, fifteen, and Cobi, twelve. She enjoys being a soccer mom and working part-time in childcare at her church. She has been published in several *Chicken Soup* books and hopes to continue writing more inspirational stories. She can be reached at j_kremer@verizon.net.

Charlotte Lanham is a frequent contributor to *Chicken Soup for the Soul* books. She is an active member of the Society of Children's Book Writers and Illustrators and has recently completed a series of eight gift books and two devotional CDs. You can contact her at charlotte.lanham@sbcglobal.net.

Mary Kathryn Lay lives with her family in Texas where she writes for magazines and books, speaks to schools and writing groups, and teaches writing. She enjoys traveling, antique shopping, and festivals. Check out www.kathrynlay.com for information on her children's novel, *CROWN ME!* and more, or e-mail her at www.rlay15@aol.com.

Barbara LoMonaco received her bachelor of science degree from the University of Southern California and taught elementary school. Since February of 1998, Barbara has worked for Chicken Soup for the Soul Enterprises, Inc. as their Story Acquisitions Manager and Customer Service representative. She is a coauthor of *Chicken Soup for the Mother and Son Soul.* Contact Barbara at blomonaco@chickensoupforthesoul.com.

Joyce Long graduated with honors in English and journalism from Ball State University and received a master of secondary education from Indiana University. Joyce enjoys traveling, gardening, golf, and reading. After teaching for nineteen years, she now works in communications for her church. You can e-mail her at longfamajcv@aol.com.

Catherine Madera lives with her husband and two children in northwest Washington. Her work has appeared in various publications, and she is a frequent contributor to the *Guideposts* family of magazines. Catherine owns two Arabian horses and is an avid equestrian. You can reach Catherine at maderam@wwdb.org.

Frances Merwin is the mother of five adult children and the grandmother of fourteen. She was a teacher for many years and since retirement has been involved in prison ministry and church work as well as working in a law office.

Roberta Messner is an inspirational writer and speaker whose work has appeared in many publications. A registered nurse, Roberta often speaks on the therapeutic value of sharing stories.

Jacquelyn Mitchard is the author of *The Deep End of the Ocean,* a *New York Times* Bestseller. She has also written six other novels, including the recently released *Cage of Stars.* Jacquelyn's essays have been widely anthologized, and she is a syndicated columnist for Tribune Media Services and a contributing editor to *Wondertime.* She and her husband live with their seven children near Madison, Wisconsin.

Barbara Nicks began writing poems soon after the birth of her first child, who is now one of her sixth grade students in east Texas. She enjoys reading, scrapbooking, and traveling with her family. She can be contacted at bnicks@email.com.

Phyllis Nutkis taught preschool and kindergarten for fifteen years before finally "graduating" in 2004. She currently works as a grant writer for a social service agency and also writes for various publications. She and her husband have three children and two grandchildren. You can contact Phyllis at Phyllis.nutkis@gmail.com.

Lydia Paiste is a visual artist based in South Portland, Maine. She received her bachelor of science from Skidmore College in 1997. She lives with her husband, artist Jeff Badger, and dog, Walter. For more information visit www.lydiapaste.com.

Jeanne Pallos is the author of several published articles for adults and children. Her workbook, *Circle of Love,* has been used by churches to help women deal with recovery issues. She lives in Laguna Niguel, California, with her husband, Andrew. She can be reached at jlpallos@cox. net.

Mark Parisi's "off the mark" comic panel has been syndicated since 1987 and is distributed by United Media. Mark's humor also graces greeting cards, T-shirts, calendars, magazines, newsletters, and books. Please vist his website at: www.offthemark.com. Lynn is his wife/business partner and their daughter, Jen, contributes with inspiration (as do three cats).

Carol Pavliska lives on a farm in south Texas with her husband and their five children. In addition to inspirational speaking and writing, she pens a family humor column called "Kidz-n-Tow." She may be reached at cpavliska@ev1.net.

Dr. Debra Peppers, a retired English teacher, university instructor, radio and television host, author, and Emmy award–winning playwright, was inducted into the prestigious National Teachers Hall of Fame. A member of the National Speakers Association, Dr. Peppers is available for bookings at 314-842-7425 or www.pepperseed.org.

Christian novelist **Perry P. Perkins** was born and raised in the Pacific Northwest. "My Oldest & Dearest" was transcribed on behalf of his mother, Betty Jean Perkins. Perry and his wife Victoria live near Woodburn, Oregon, where he is hard at work on the second novel in the trilogy: *Shoalwater Voices*. More of Perry's work can be found at www.perryperkinsbooks.com

Stephanie Piro lives in New Hampshire with her husband, daughter, and three cats. She is one of King Features' team of women cartoonists, "Six Chix." (She is the Saturday chick!) Her single panel, "Fair Game," appears in newspapers and on her website at www.stephaniepiro.com. She also designs gift items for her company Strip T's. Contact her at piro@worldpath.net or by mail at P.O. Box 605, Farmington, NH 03835.

Allison Pittman is the author of *Ten Thousand Charms*, the first in the *Crossroads of Grace* Series from Multnomah Publishers. She is co-president of the Christian Writers Group of San Antonio and serves as director of her church's Theater Arts Group. Allison and her husband Mike have three sons.

Robert C. Raina studied art at the University of Massachusetts at Amherst. He is a cartoonist and has written and illustrated several books for children. Robert is the president and owner of a full time entertainment company located in western Massachusetts (bobrainadj.com). He can be contacted at robertraina@cox.net and his writing and artwork can be viewed at bobrainawriting.com. This is his first published work.

Carol McAdoo Rehme, a prolific author and editor for *Chicken Soup*, thanks heaven for little girls—for pigtails and cartwheels, dance shoes and diamonds, and now, for the babies her daughters are having. Carol directs a nonprofit, Vintage Voices, Inc., which brings interactive programming to the vulnerable elderly. You can contact her at carol@rehme.com or www.rehme.com.

Cheryl Riggs holds a masters in Gerontology from University of Southern California and is a certified Senior Advisor. During 2008, she plans to complete a fifty-state trip to celebrate her fiftieth birthday, during which she will also market her LifeCheck Vital Information System. You can contact her at ckriggs@juno.com.

Sallie A. Rodman's work has appeared in many *Chicken Soup* anthologies and on Chicken Soup dog food bags. Her favorite time is spending the day with her husband, grown children, and grandchildren. She enjoys reading and making her own jewelry when she isn't working for a local councilwoman. You can contact her at sa.rodman@verizon.net.

Marilyn M. Ross received a BSE in elementary—special education from Arkansas State University in 1970. She teaches special education in Manassas, Virginia. Lynn writes poetry, creates albums, and enjoys photography. Married to Bob for thirty-eight years, she has a son, John, a daughter, Lori, and a grandson, Alex. You can contact her at llross@comcast.net.

Jean West Rudnicki is a freelance writer living in Houston, Texas. She is an avid adventurer and explorer delving into the great wonders and mysteries of life and the world that surrounds us. She writes feature stories, inspirational prose, and personal essays. Please e-mail her at jean@jeanwestrudnicki.com.

Donna Savage is a pastor's wife, writer, and speaker living in Las Vegas, Nevada. She believes that each day brings new opportunities to see God's love and power and to share his encouragement with others. Donna and her husband, Hoyt, have two sons. You can contact her at donnasavagelv@cox.net.

Harriet May Savitz is a member of Mothers Supporting Daughters with Breast Cancer and an award-winning author of reissued groundbreaking books about the disabled, including her book *Run, Don't Walk,* which was made into an *ABC After School Special* and produced by Henry Winkler. She also has written a book of essays, *More Than Ever: A View From My 70s,* and *Hello Grandparents! Wherever You Are.* You can visit her website at www.harrietmaysavitz.com.

Joanne Schulte has a bachelor of arts from California State University at Fullerton, California. She is the mother of a blended family of seven grown children. She enjoys serving and speaking in the Women's Ministries at her church, and in her free time, she enjoys writing, music, and gardening.

JoAnn Semones lives in the coastal town of Half Moon Bay, California. Her stories have appeared in national maritime history, health, and environmental publications. JoAnn is completing a book about shipwrecks near Pigeon Point Lighthouse. Please e-mail her at HMBJoAnn@aol.com.

Jodi Lynn Severson earned a bachelor's degree from the University of Pittsburgh. She resides in Wisconsin with her husband and three children. As a freelance biographer, her work has been published in *U.S. Legacies* magazine, and in *Chicken Soup for the Sister's Soul, Chicken Soup for the Working Woman's Soul, Chicken Soup for the Girlfriend's Soul,* and *Chicken Soup for the Shopper's Soul.* You can reach her at jodis@charter.net.

Kathy Shaskan is a writer and artist from New Jersey.

Helaine Silver lives with her best friend—her daughter—just northwest of Chicago. With a degree in music performance, and working as a business analyst, she enjoys music, long walks, cooking, and gardening and tries to write in whatever spare time she can find. Helaine can be reached at hey263@hotmail.com.

Margie Sims is a freelance writer and the mother of eight children. She lives with her family in Vermont's Champlain Valley, where she still misses her mother's face. Please e-mail her at hsms1@aol.com.

Sally Singingtree is a gifted musician, holistic psychotherapist, interfaith minister and healthcare chaplain. She is the mother of three children. For more information visit her website at www.prairiespirit.net.

Christine Smith is fifty-six, has been married for thirty-eight years, has three children, thirteen grandchildren, and numerous foster children. Her stories have been published in two previous *Chicken Soup for the Soul* books, *Woman's World* magazine, *Heartwarmers,* and monthly in a foster care newsletter. Her passions are children, writing, and serving God. You can contact Christine at iluvmyfamilyxxx000@yahoo.com.

Jennifer L. Smith teaches high school English and has been happily married to her husband, Craig, for three years. They just discovered that she will be giving birth to their first child in May! Look for her first published children's book, *Things I Wonder,* at www.hisworkpub.com.

Judy Spence still laughs when she recalls the weekend that she, her sister, and her mom attempted a healthier life style. She is grateful that they shared several more vacations before her mother, Roma, died in March 2006. "The memories of those trips are precious, especially now that Mom is gone."

Joyce Stark lives in northeast Scotland but travels widely in the United States and Europe. Recently retired from working in the local government, she is now concentrating on a book about her travels in the States and a children's book geared toward teaching young children Spanish. You can contact her at joric.stark@virgin.net.

Kelly Starling Lyons is a Pittsburgh native, journalist, and children's book author. Her picture book, *One Million Men and Me* (Just Us Books), debuted February 2007. She dedicates this *Chicken Soup* story to her mom, Deborah Starling-Pollard. Kelly lives in North Carolina with her husband and daughter. You can visit her website at www.kellystarlinglyons.com.

Suzanne Strempek Shea lives and walks in western Massachusetts. She is the author of five novels, including *Becoming Finola,* and two memoirs, including *Songs From a Lead-Lined Room: Notes—High and Low—From My Journey Through Breast Cancer and Radiation.* For details, please visit www.suzannestrempekshea.com.

Glorianne M. Swenson is a Minnesota-based freelance writer and small business owner of Gloribks. Her genre includes creative nonfiction memoirs, devotionals, poetry, and children's picture book manuscripts. She is a wife, mother, and grandmother and enjoys singing, speaking, piano, genealogy, and antiquing. You can contact her at gloribks@charter.net.

Lanie Tankard is a freelance editor and writer in Austin, Texas. An Ohio native, she holds two journalism degrees. Lanie is the mother of three wonderful daughters and the daughter of one fine mother. She can be reached at etankard@aol.com.

Tsgoyna Tanzman is a *Chicken Soup* contributor and author of numerous articles and essays for books and newspapers. Tsgoyna now claims mother-wife as her career of choice. Additionally, she volunteers as a Speaker/Child Safety Educator and director of Characters Come Alive, a program bringing historical characters to life in elementary classrooms. You can contact her at tnzmn@cox.net.

A first time mom at forty-one, **Stephanie Welcher Thompson** now understands what a blessing motherhood is. She is a frequent contributor to *Guideposts* publications and *Chicken Soup.* She enjoys writing and speaking about family experiences with husband, Michael, and their three-year-old daughter Micah. Reach her at: P.O. Box 1502, Edmond, OK 73083 or stephanie@stateofchange.net.

Lynne M. Thompson is published in numerous magazines and book collections and is a regular contributor to *Focus on the Family* publications, where she can be heard on their *Focus Family Weekend* radio broadcast. She resides in California's Central Valley, with her husband and their two children. Visit her at www.lynnethompson.net.

Andrew Toos has established a national reputation through his off-beat lifestyle cartoons for clients such as: *Reader's Digest, Saturday Evening Post, Gallery, Stern, Accountancy, Baseball Digest, CEO, The Washington Post, Barron's, Bayer Corp, Good Housekeeping, Cosmopolitan,* and many other titles and media outlets. His work is licensed through CartoonResource.com. Andrew lives with his wife, Nancy, in Florida.

Ani Tuzman writes prose and poetry. She directs Dance of the Letters Writing Center, guiding groups and individual writers to experience joy and self-discovery through writing. She is completing a novel based on the life of the eighteenth-century mystic Baal Shem Tov. You can contact her at dance.letters@verizon.net.

Heidi Washburn is a craniosacral therapist, massage therapist, college instructor, and freelance writer. She believes in the healing power of storytelling and is dedicated to her own and other people's healing through sharing and expression of our life stories. She lives near Woodstock, New York, and can be reached at heidiwashburn@hvc.rr.com.

Mamie Amato Weiss received her Bachelor of Arts from Kean University in 1980. She is currently enrolled in a Master's Program for Educational Leadership. Mamie aspires to be an elementary school principal. She is married and has three lovely daughters. She enjoys the arts, reading, writing, traveling, relaxing on the beach, playing the piano, and organizing fund-raisers for underpriviledged children.

Billie L. White lives in the community of Needmore located in south central Pennsylvania with her husband, two daughters, and three cats. She works for the federal government and is taking classes at Wilson College. Billie enjoys gardening and writing about memories and observations of life. Please e-mail her at blw1967@gmail.com.

June Williams lives in Brush Prairie, Washington, with Mac, her husband of forty years. Together they enjoy camping with their grandchildren in the beautiful Pacific Northwest. June loves to write her family's stories for publication in books, magazines, and newspapers.

Freelancer **Betty Winslow** is from Ohio, where she runs a K-8 school library. She's the mother of four, and when she's not writing, she's reading, crocheting, jewelry making, singing, or talking. (Her husband of thirty-three years would say that talking ought to come higher on the list.) You can contact her at bettyw@wcnet.org.

Rebecca Yauger lives in Texas with her husband and two children. Her work has been published in *Guideposts* magazine, and she recently won first place in a regional short fiction contest. A member of American Christian Fiction Writers, Rebecca is currently at work on two novels. You can contact her at texaswriter@ev1.net.